"I love this book; I hate this book. I love this book because Brian's longing heart is so big he can write a sentence like 'God's vision for his church is so magnificent, so beautiful, that we can never leave it without leaving him.' I hate this book because it might encourage disillusioned people to leave the church—and as Brian says, that would be leaving God behind too. But if you're wrestling with the church, Brian is a great wrestling coach."

KEVIN A. MILLER, *executive vice president and publisher, Christianity Today International*

"There is a growing awareness of the extent of the 'back door' problem facing many churches. It is often assumed that church leavers represent either the disgruntled transferring to other churches or those who have abandoned their Christian faith. In reality, many are leaving churches out of disillusionment and frustration to continue their spiritual pilgrimage. Brian Sanders tackles this important topic with a clear, analytical mind. He identifies the complex process of leaving a church, and suggests practical ways it can be done in a responsible manner. Most important of all, he argues that leaving must lead to a fresh vision and renewed commitment to Christ, community and the kingdom of God."

EDDIE GIBBS, *author,* ChurchNext *and* Emerging Churches

"I'm blown away by *Life After Church*. I've never yet seen a book of its kind that addresses those who 'stay' in church *and* those who leave! It's a significant book."

MIKE MORRELL, *editor,* The Ooze, *and MSF Graduate Fellow, Regent University*

"For anyone who really believes Christ is Lord and head of the church, this book is a real roller coaster. At first I found myself angry and defensive in response to Sanders's critique, and yet I also found myself resonating with his deep longing for the church to be more. For those of us staying, Sanders and his 'leavers' articulate important questions. They are critical questions for the leaders of any church that desires to be faithful to its Christ-given mission and relevant to a new generation."

CANDIE BLANKMAN, *pastor, First Presbyterian Church, Downey, California*

"Hopeful, prophetic, Brian Sanders speaks for the many among us who long for the kingdom of God—but find ourselves frustrated by the church as we know it. In *Life After Church* he offers a gentle, constructive and hopeful vision of how we can reform ourselves as a body to be the hands and feet of Jesus in our world. Simple but not simplistic, prophetic but not angry, Brian's writing is honest about the struggle to live authentic faith, striking a careful balance between honoring the past and inviting us to imagine what could be."

MARK A. SCANDRETTE, *author,* Soul Graffiti, *and executive director and cofounder, ReIMAGINE!*

LIFE
AFTER
CHURCH

God's Call to
Disillusioned
Christians

BRIAN SANDERS

IVP Books

An imprint of InterVarsity Press
Downers Grove, Illinois

InterVarsity Press
P.O. Box 1400, Downers Grove, IL 60515-1426
World Wide Web: www.ivpress.com
E-mail: email@ivpress.com

InterVarsity Press® is the book-publishing division of InterVarsity Christian Fellowship/USA®, a student movement active on campus at hundreds of universities, colleges and schools of nursing in the United States of America, and a member movement of the International Fellowship of Evangelical Students. For information about local and regional activities, write Public Relations Dept., InterVarsity Christian Fellowship/USA, 6400 Schroeder Rd., P.O. Box 7895, Madison, WI 53707-7895, or visit the IVCF website at <www.intervarsity.org>.

All Scripture quotations, unless otherwise indicated, are taken from the Holy Bible, New International Version®. NIV®. Copyright ©1973, 1978, 1984 by International Bible Society. Used by permission of Zondervan Publishing House. All rights reserved.

The comments of various leavers throughout the book are included by permission.

Design: Matt Smith

ISBN 978-0-8308-3606-2

Printed in the United States of America ∞

Library of Congress Cataloging-in-Publication Data

Sanders, Brian, 1972-
  Life after church: God's call to disillusioned Christians / Brian
Sanders.
      p. cm.
  Includes bibliographical references.
  ISBN-13: 978-0-8308-3606-2 (pbk.: alk. paper)
  1. Church membership. 2. Ex-church members. 3.
  Non-church-affiliated people. I. Title.
  BV820.S36 2007
  262.001'7—dc22

                                                        2007026758

P   17   16   15   14   13   12   11   10   9   8   7   6   5   4   3   2   1

Y   21   20   19   18   17   16   15   14   13   12   11   10   09   08   07

To Dell deChant and teachers like him,

who plant the seeds of possibility.

CONTENTS

AN INTRODUCTION TO
LEAVING THE CHURCH

I've always appreciated a good trade. The summer before my fourteenth birthday, I sat under a tree at a Young Life camp and contemplated the gospel as I understood it: all my weakness, all my insecurities, all my nothingness in exchange for an eternal friendship with God. I knew I was being offered forgiveness too, but at that time I think I was more amazed by the offer of purpose. Could God really use a hyper, underachieving kid like me? I was the product of brokenness, inside me and outside, and the consensus was that I would not amount to anything.

But I knew what I had to do. It was like that feeling you get when you're about to strike a deal for a house or a car or something in a market and the seller is offering a price so low you struggle to contain yourself. You put on the serious face of negotiation, understating your approval, saying, "Okay, I think I can live with that price," while inside you're doing cartwheels. That is how I felt that evening under that tree. Could God really offer me so much for so little? My broken life for his inside me? It felt too good to be true. But I've since learned that God is exceedingly good, that he is both too good and too true. So, I was born anew, into a family of people I had never met.

God had given me purpose and new life. Inside, I was instantly transformed. I began to believe that I might actually

amount to something after all. As a member of God's family, I
assumed I was a part of the greatest organization the world
could know. Since we all had made the same trade, we were all,
I assumed, destined for great things. All of us had traded our
mediocrity for something greater, something other people
only dreamed of.

Then I went to church. And the worship was archaic and
confusing. When God was being talked about, no one asked
questions, but I had so many questions. The people were
friendly and there were activities for everyone, but I did not
need activities. No one seemed to be living in the light of the
great trade. I confess, I just went along, waiting for something
to click. I stood when they said to, I sat when they said to, I re-
cited the prayers and came and went on time. But something,
even then I knew, was missing.

The Elusive Church

So much has changed since those first days of church for me.
I've been to other churches, tried various traditions, felt the vi-
brancy of a new church experience and then again the lifeless-
ness. Sometimes I was convinced it was just me. *I'm too critical,
or I'm too distracted,* I thought. Other times, I was sure there
was still something missing.

For a long time I defined church as that place people go on
Sunday mornings. Then I thought of the church as something
universal, invisible. But secretly I wondered if there was something in-between, the local expression of something holy, the
gathering of the destined, of those who had accepted the
trade.

Going to the place called church remained a central feature of my spiritual life. Yet as a college student trying to live
radically for God on a large, secular campus, it began to feel
like a pointless exercise. In those years, I went every week and
sometimes twice a week because I loved to worship and I

wanted to be close to God. But the call that my friends and I felt to preach the gospel on campus, the intense, impromptu prayer gatherings, the crying out for more of God and for the rescue of our friends and our campus—it all ruined us for platitudes.

I went on to join InterVarsity Christian Fellowship, a parachurch ministry that was gathering students to pray, study the Bible and reach out to the campus. That made sense to me. My InterVarsity staff worker told me I still needed to "find a church." So I did. And I liked it. But the more seriously I took the Bible, the more I saw in Scripture a very certain call to proclaim a gospel of transformation, a revolutionary gospel, the more I saw what I was doing on Sunday mornings as, well, unrevolutionary. We simply were not impacting anyone by sequestering ourselves in a building and preaching to each other truths we all already believed. There were parts I still liked: seeing my friends, the music, listening to the Word. But I began to wonder about the nature of church, and I began to see church as extraneous to ministry.

After college, I took a ministry position with InterVarsity, got married and welcomed five amazing kids into my world. By faith I moved my family into inner-city Tampa and began forming an intentional community. We bought two houses and committed ourselves to one another and the kingdom of God in what, at the time, was one of the hardest neighborhoods in our city. We loved and prayed and reached out. God began to shape for me a theology that included the poor. We wrestled with the racial rift in America, repented of our contribution and committed ourselves to the cause of reconciliation. I began traveling, taking students and adults to serve and learn from the poor all over the world. I've done ministry and met the poor in a dozen nations; in each place and in each encounter I've grown more weary of the kind of church we have settled for.

Blessed Are the Leavers

This book is personal. Some have argued that teachers ought to be unbiased, that real science is dispassionate and objective. While I agree that the truth ought to be pursued objectively, once it's ascertained it has to be lived with utter abandon. I'm not unbiased, because God has changed my mind about so many things. I believe the church can and should be more. And I'm ready to accept the possibility that leaving and starting over may be what God is calling some of us to do. I have enough humility to know that about most of these things I may be wrong, but not all.

I cannot write as an academic, because I don't know enough. I cannot write as a historian, because I haven't seen enough. I cannot write as a sociologist, because I remain intimately connected to the subject matter. And I don't write this book as a theologian but as a practitioner of theology. I'm a believer. I'm a leaver. I'm a leader and a church planter. For love and in the pursuit of God and his kingdom, I've become an ecclesiologist, and I'm longing for the church to be more.

This book is for those who have contemplated leaving church because they believe it should be more. This book is for those who have moved from thinking about it to doing, and now they find themselves isolated, ineffective or alone. This book is for people who have made the trade and who are looking for a community of people who know they have a destiny because of it. This book is for people who have secretly longed for the church to arise and take its place as the single most transformative force in the world we know.

1

LEAVING FOR GOOD
Looking for Jesus Outside the Exits

*T*he question is, what does the Holy Spirit want you to do?" The preacher's words woke me from my usual sermon daze. I can't remember what that particular sermon was even about, only that this was the final question punctuating some point about some spiritual idea too abstract for me to remember. What was gripping about this particular question on this particular Sunday morning was the answer that was ringing in my ears. For me the question was not rhetorical, and I could not seem to shake the overwhelming response repeating in my brain: "Leave!"

Could the Holy Spirit really want me to leave? I did the usual theological gymnastics: it must just be my own sin; it must be my cynicism; going to church every week is the bare minimum for a committed Christian; "Let us not give up meeting together, as some are in the habit of doing" (Hebrews 10:25). How could God be calling me to disobey his own Word? What is wrong with me?

I can't count how many services I've sat through utterly bored. I realize that my Attention Deficit Disorder is a factor, but I still can't fathom what it is about traditional church services that people like. All of it seems so tedious to me—on the best days tolerable, on the worst painful. And I love God. My heart burns for his kingdom. There are nights when I can't sleep because my kingdom dreams won't let me.

It's as if the intensity of my burning for God and frustration with church grow in proportion to each other, as if they are somehow the same thing. Or at least they are related to the same longing. My heart burns like those of the travelers on the road to Emmaus, who walked with Jesus. My life is like that. I know what it's like to sit with my community looking back at yesterday, last week and last year, as we shake our heads and ask each other, "Were not our hearts burning within us?" (Luke 24:32). Except, it seems, when I go to church.

Do I alone live with this apparent contradiction? I don't think so. The pastor's question was a good one. What *does* the Holy Spirit want you to do? The Hebrew and Greek languages (languages used in the Bible) both translate *Spirit* to mean "breath" or "wind." Both words imply life, the life that comes from the breath of God. God's Spirit, his breath on and in us, is creative, free and unpredictable. We are, as the church of Jesus, being called to life in the Spirit. In part, this is why I will never understand the fascination with a predictable, unremarkable church where one week is always the same as the next. Spiritual boredom is an oxymoron; it should be an impossible contradiction. What is from the Spirit is never boring, because it represents the breath of God in our lives.

> *Church used to be exciting to go to. It's not like they did anything different back then, but I guess it was new and we were younger and hadn't heard these sermons. But as the years have gone by it seems a bit like Groundhog Day. The same kind of teaching every week, the same worship style, the same prayers.*
>
> DAVE

Here are some of the thoughts I struggled with before I became a leaver:

I feel like a hypocrite. I have no connection to this place or these people anymore. I've become the thing that I most despise: a pew warmer, what Jesus called "whitewashed tombs" (Matthew 23:27). I'm performing religious duties out of obligation and no heart. I'm not sure I even agree with what is being said anymore. But I don't have anyone to talk to about it. We all just come and listen but we don't ever do anything, we don't know each other, we don't communicate.

Didn't James say that faith without works is dead? Is not true religion caring for the orphan and widow? We don't seem to do that. We don't even talk about doing that. We don't even think about talking about doing that. What purpose do I serve here? Could it really be that I'm only wanted here because of my tithe potential?

But you know what they say: no church is perfect. I'm not perfect. I ought to just stay. I will probably come back next week. But I don't want to. Besides, if I leave, where will I go? Is that really you, Lord?

The question that awakened this internal conversation in me that day is a variation on the question that this book will address: Is it really possible that God might be actually leading Christians to leave church? Certainly people leave churches every day for myriad reasons.

Escape Routes

For as long as there have been churches, people have left them. When I talk about leaving, I don't mean looking for another church. I'm not talking about leaving the experience of church as we know it. Leavers aren't leaving *one* particular church. They are leaving church itself.

It's part of the corporate experience to see some join and others leave, whether through death, disaffection or waning faith. There may have been a time when one had to resist considerable sociocultural pressure to leave the church. Not so now. Yet still today, many people want to leave but don't. Some are loyalists, committed to the church's leader or even the building itself. Others are theologically constrained; their understanding of the Bible forbids them to leave.

Many people leave in another way. They are physically present, perhaps every week. Yet they construct a hollow, heartless kind of church that merely tolerates what was meant to be the zenith of worship, community and mission in the life of believers. Instead of a living, vibrant community, a body if you will, church and its gatherings become a congregation of jaded, bitter people, bearing all kinds of unholy fruit and ultimately damaging the name of Jesus in the neighborhoods where they gather. Still, for some, the social and internal pressure to stay outweighs these.

For others, especially in American culture, there is another motivation for leaving. In a world defined by consumption, churches have also become consumable. The process of deciding on or continuing with a church is more like deciding what toothpaste to buy than deciding whom to marry (though even that metaphor tends to fall flat, given the perishable nature of marriage in this same cultural current). We tend to stay loyal as long as the advertised promises are kept and we see the personal results that we pay for. Church has be-

> *Sometimes I feel like I would get as much out of staying at home as going, or better yet fishing or reading a good book. I might experience truth at the very least—more than the morning at church. It just feels like one more thing on my week of things to do and there is a lack of joy associated with it, an obligation moreso.*
>
> CRYSTAL

come more and more a matter of cash transfer for services. This means that church is now relegated to the margins of choice; it's an option in a sea of options that vie for our time and money (albeit limited) and it proposes to offer something of value in return.

So people aren't particularly brand loyal when it comes to church. I know Christians who are more committed to always buying a Honda than they are to a particular gathering of believers. While this is a real problem, church shopping to find a more palatable or fashionable church isn't what I want to address.

Unfortunately, there is a more profoundly disturbing defection happening in Western churches: for more and more people, church itself is a failed experiment. Many have tried enough churches to come to the conclusion that they should not go at all. What they once hoped would nurture a growing relationship with God and foster deep bonds of friendship and community with the people of God has actually served to suffocate both enterprises, causing sincere Christians to consider leaving as the only healthy course. Let us be clear, we are talking about people who, while far from perfect, are deeply committed to Jesus Christ and his mission. They are, in many cases, also so committed to the church (invisible) that they feel like imposters in the local church expressions they have attended and feel that they are leaving on principle.

Leaving Church in Pursuit of God

When church leaders and others reduce the reasons for leaving to spiritual apathy or loss of faith, the church loses its opportunity to see its impotence and the bold and prophetic nature of the leaving done by those who are still committed to Jesus Christ and his mission. I'm talking about people who are leaving the church but not God. It's very important to establish from the outset that when I refer to leavers, I'm not talking about people who leave churches because they are immature or angry at the pastor or didn't get the position on the leadership team that they wanted. I'm not talking about people who are leaving one church in search of a better one. For some people, this is all they need. They are frustrated with their church, so they need to find a healthier one. But what happens when all the churches near us have the same problem? What if every church we attend leaves us struggling and not encouraged?

When I talk about leavers, I'm talking about a group that's difficult to dismiss. They are leaving (though never leaving perfectly) in their pursuit of God. These are people who want to do what is right and to live in a way that honors Jesus bringing the kingdom into the world around them. These are people who want to worship God with their whole lives, want to live in community with other believers and want to be a part of God's mission in the world. These are people who are trying to follow Jesus, and part of what they are saying is that for them to stay and to remain faithful to Jesus are mutually exclusive.

This is the disturbing paradox with which we must wrestle in this book. In the final analysis, for leavers, it isn't a problem with God but a problem with the organization of God. Still, many leavers aren't sure what to do. Some stay (even though internally they have left), others leave bitterly and wounded, and many end up isolated, having escaped one kind of incongruence only to adopt another.

This book isn't meant as a critique of the church. It is a book for leavers. However, for many leavers the sense of isolation and failed reform is what drives us away from each other and from re-forming the church. I would love to arrest that process. We are critiquing the church with our longing for something more. I don't want to be critical but to dream of more. Leavers want to dream in a way that builds something and not criticize in a way that only tears something down.

Leavers first need to know that they aren't alone. One estimate places the figure at 55,000 people a week leaving Western churches. They also need to know that their concerns are real and in many cases even prophetic. Finally, they need to know what to do with their confusion, with their concerns and ultimately with their talent-soaked lives. Who are we? What are our concerns? How can we stay fully faithful to the God who himself exists in community and calls us his church?

Leaving in Stages

Leaving happens in stages. I believe that there are thousands of Christians who will be able to identify themselves beyond the first stages of this continuum, giving each of us a context in which to place our own experience (see page 20). Leaving is a process of coming to terms with disaffection. Every leaver seems to come to what Alan Jamieson calls a "turning point" event, or what could be considered the last straw. In his book *A Churchless Faith*, Jamieson describes the process of leaving through a series of interviews with Christians who have been significantly involved in and then left their churches. He discovered that for most of them there is a moment when they simply could not take it anymore. One leaver called it "my moment of truth."

For me it was a Sunday morning, sitting bored and listening to the pastor talk about how much money they had spent on remodeling the bathrooms because the style in which they were decorated needed to be updated. I knew at that moment that would be my last Sunday. Yet the feelings of frustration and disaffection had been going on for months, if not years. Usually these single events are the catalyst sending us into a new phase, yet they are merely a culmination of a series of similar and related events or realizations. While the diagram designates these stages in equal increments, the duration of each will be different for each person and each stage in some cases can last twenty years or twenty days. Further, some people may never leave a stage.

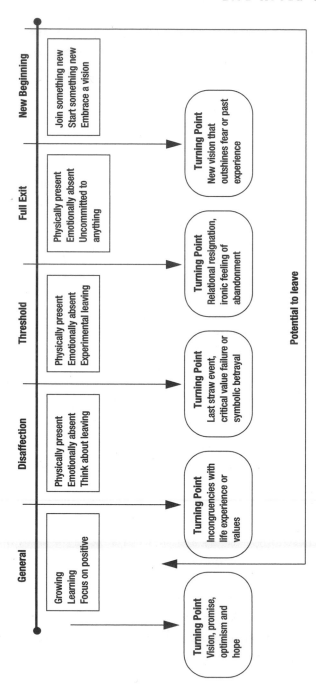

General

Growing
Learning
Focus on positive

Turning Point
Vision, promise, optimism and hope

Disaffection

Physically present
Emotionally absent
Think about leaving

Turning Point
Incongruencies with life experience or values

Threshold

Physically present
Emotionally absent
Experimental leaving

Turning Point
Last straw event, critical value failure or symbolic betrayal

Full Exit

Physically present
Emotionally absent
Uncommitted to anything

Turning Point
Relational resignation, ironic feeling of abandonment

New Beginning

Join something new
Start something new
Embrace a vision

Turning Point
New vision that outshines fear or past experience

Potential to leave

Leaving Happens in Stages

Obviously, if someone were to live his whole life in the contentment stage, that would be ideal. More tragic would be the leaver who finally lives alone in the exit stage. There is no guarantee that a person will progress from one to the next. Yet many people will not only go through all of these stages at one point but, sadly, also will repeat the cycle many times.

Contentment. This stage is marked by hope and guarded optimism about the people and possibilities that a new church offers. Many Christians experience a new church in the light of their "old" church, finding the differences exhilarating. Those people who have been to multiple churches before entering into this phase will tend to stay for less time. Those whose initial conversion to Christ occured in connection to a particular church will likely stay there longer because they have no other point of reference for comparison, their faith in Jesus is strongly tied to the life and practice of that church, and they are naturally less cynical about the church.

You may know people who seem to be in this stage for many years, if not their whole life. Learning and growing characterize it. People in this stage tend to focus their attention on the positive and are willing to overlook what they see as imperfections in the church, because of the experience they are having and the positive impact they see that the church has had.

I hesitate to call this phase the honeymoon, because it can last a very long time, and in the best of churches it does. I also want to be careful not to imply that anyone in particular will leave this stage or that every church eventually needs to be left. But this stage is like a honeymoon in that the relationship is still untested and is mostly characterized by optimism and an appreciation of the strengths (real or imagined) of the church. This can be contrasted to later stages when the overwhelming negatives that the person is wrestling with obscure those same positive attributes.

Disaffection. Churchgoers don't become disaffected overnight. As I will address later, leavers tend to marshal a number of common critiques at this stage. Sometimes triggered by a crisis or simply by the natural maturation and development of the Christian, this stage is characterized by a sense of inconsistency between the reality of the leaver's season of life and the church's emphases, programs and values. Those same emphases that were once so helpful become less so, and in some cases seem hollow or clichéd.

For example, when someone first makes a commitment to Jesus, the admonition to pray and believe can be a new and powerful concept. Exploring the possibility that we can pray and ask God for anything in his name and he will grant it is an amazing experience. The new believer then goes on an adventure in prayer, testing her new faith and often seeing that Jesus is real and alive and responding to her heartfelt prayers. Certainly she experiences some failures and doubts, but since she's so young in her faith she chalks them up to lack of faith.

That pray-and-believe message heard through the experience of a relatively new believer is very different when heard through the experience of a second-stage Christian. Perhaps this believer just lost his thirty-five-year-old wife to cancer. And while they prayed fervently, confessed sin, believed with all they had for a healing, the battle was lost. And now this widower sits under the same teaching, wondering about ques-

> *Growing up in church was more of a social thing, at least when I was very young, so I was never really disappointed in what I found inside those walls. It felt like school, there wasn't really anywhere for me to fit in, I just kind of floated. I guess as I began to mature, I began to feel like something was missing.*
>
> KIM

tions that don't ever seem to find their way into the curriculum. He has to swallow harder the same message of faith and prayer uncomplicated by the reality of too much life lived.

Other times the trigger to this stage is an alteration in the apparent values of a church. It becomes clear to the leaver that what has been taught and established is just words that carry with them little or no action. Or the church begins to move away from values that felt to the leaver like promises.

One church I attended for years talked about serving the poor, something to which I was very committed. I felt immediately at home in this church because they often talked about the need to help people who are "less fortunate." They also had a program that served a hot meal to the homeless on Sunday afternoons. Many of these homeless people, if not all, attended the Sunday-morning worship service (a fact which greatly encouraged me at first). However, over time I learned that the lunch was served only to those who came to the service beforehand and that those who were late would not be served. Those that did attend worship sat in the back two rows of the church, and almost none of the congregation interacted with them. These disheveled seekers were looking for food but needed more. However, no one ever sat in the rows where they sat, and during the greeting time, no one would go back to greet them. The congregation did not practice the value that was espoused from the front nor was it given much emphasis in the practice of the leaders. This realization took time but contributed to my growing sense of disaffection.

People in this stage are leavers in their own right. Many churchgoers share the concerns of the leavers and are themselves contemplating leaving but simply have not done so yet. And they may not. While we may not ever be able to identify them as leavers, I would like to include them in the discussion because their concerns are the same, and in many ways (though not physically) they have left.

Threshold. This stage is usually characterized by the final disillusionment over a critical value or a betrayal (symbolic or
otherwise) that simply cannot be overlooked. In the disaffection stage, the leaver is physically present but emotionally absent, but in the threshold stage, the leaver is physically absent
but emotionally still connected, perhaps even more. The leaver
has finally decided to stop attending church events. What
makes this stage different from the next (closing the door) is
that the leaver is still connected emotionally to the church.

Whether consciously or unconsciously, the leaver is hoping
that his absence will elicit a response from the church and perhaps even catalyze change. People have difficulty believing
that they don't matter at all. Often years of tithing, participation and emotional loyalty creates a bond between the church
(its people, its leaders and even the building itself) and the
leaver, so that he expects his absence not only to be noticed
but also looked into. In short, he hopes that someone will
come after him. One older study conducted by Dr. John Savage
recorded the "dropout patterns" of four midsize churches and
found that most of the people who had left waited six to eight
weeks to see if anyone would come and find out why they'd
left. He also recorded that in 100 percent of the cases, no one
ever did.

In my case, I genuinely believed I would be missed. I waited
for a phone call from the pastor, whom I considered a personal
friend and colleague in ministry, but waited in vain. You might
be wondering why I didn't simply go and make my grievances
known to the leaders of the church? It does seem childish to
leave angry and pout, waiting for someone to come and check
on you. Leavers often do speak to the leaders about their concerns. Sometimes these concerns are heard and no action is
taken. Sometimes there is a disagreement over the concerns.
But in other cases, leavers don't want to cause a problem. Pastors, in particular, are overcriticized and blamed for every-

thing, and I knew my pastor was under terrible strain leading his large congregation. I also knew that he was not going to be able to make many of the changes I hoped for. For these reasons I chose to leave quietly, a choice that many leavers adopt.

I did receive a call from my pastor. I had been anticipating it for weeks, and I was ready. I decided that, if he asked me where I had been or why I had left, I would be honest (loving first, but honest). To my surprise, he never did. He just asked me how I was doing and how my ministry was going. I answered, fully expecting him to ask more. It ended amiably and we have not talked again.

Closing the door. The amount of time spent in the threshold stage will vary depending on the leaver, the church and the circumstances. The leaving is complete once the door has been completely closed emotionally and the leaver no longer hopes for someone to come calling.

This is perhaps the most disconcerting stage. There is so much failure to work through: the failure of the church to satisfy someone who is genuinely longing after the heart of God, the failure to deepen relational bonds to the point where reconciliation (of ideas) is pursued at all costs. Finding a place to lay blame is an elusive enterprise, so for now we will simply identify the phenomenon. Again, it's possible for a leaver to remain in this stage for many years, even the rest of her life. Most, in time, will venture out again into the world of church (some only to cycle through the same disheartening process of disaffection and exit).

One problem we will discuss in detail later is that the structure of church itself isn't conducive to the embodiment of certain values. This doubt about church and the feeling of being burned is very real for the leaver in this stage. He isn't likely to rush back into a church environment unless he feels that the context carries with it enough promise for change.

I've known dozens of people who have lingered in this

stage, often being misunderstood and criticized for forsaking fellowship and running away from God. Some will succumb to the guilt of leaving church and still overassociate their personal relationship with Jesus with their regular attendance at a Sunday-morning service. Yet this isn't the way most leavers see it. Many feel they have done what they needed to do. Their suspicion about organized church expression is often accompanied by a new tenacious desire to be connected to Christianity in general. Many leavers become faithful to Christian television or radio. They frequent Christian bookstores, perhaps compensating for lost church relationships. Some even go out of their way to stay connected to one or two Christians who are in the same stage, commiserating about the church and grievances to which they seem to be inextricably bound.

While many leavers will still remain faithful to evangelism and what they see as living their faith, they are obviously inhibited by an absence of accountability and connection to a corporate mission (something many of them did without as members of local congregations). For those of you currently in this stage, I want to ask you to take heart, read on and know that there is a place for you in the kingdom community. Your gifts, your passion for God, your way of seeing the world, even your flaws are needed. Jesus has not stopped loving you nor has he stopped calling you into community and alongside him in his mission. There is hope.

New beginning. I've dedicated the last section of this book to this final stage. It's a stage that some leavers never reach, but it's the most hopeful and is filled with the promise of the kingdom. I'm convinced that many leavers are leaving their churches for very good reasons. In fact, I wonder if a mass exodus from certain kinds of churches isn't precisely what is needed. Yet leaving, on its own, produces nothing. Perhaps the leaver is now less tortured, but in terms of the kingdom and fruit for the gospel, what does leaving actually accomplish?

Many leavers leave because they believe in something more for the church, something closer to what Jesus taught. If we remain idle or jaded, we fail the hope that has been deposited in us. Leaving may be a necessary first step, but it's just that—the first step. The next is to find a vision that we can embrace and that reflects who we are and the sensibilities that God has given us. If we can't find that nearby, we ought to start it from scratch. Leavers need to re-form church expressions so that we make sense of them and are consistent with the biblical values God has imprinted on our hearts. The "new beginning" stage is about finding hope and learning to trust again. The turning point for the leaver moving into this stage is the hearing of new vision that outshines the fear and cynicism of the past.

In spite of (and perhaps because of) my missionary work outside the church, I became a leaver. I can vividly remember many of these stages. I remember reading Jamieson's book and identifying with so much of it—the growing frustration, the lack of voice, the mounting irrelevance, the perceived lack of substance, my turning point, the last straw—that all of these constructs are very personal to me. Having been through that experience, just reading his book and hearing my own frustrations echoed by so many was healing for me. I hope that this book also serves that purpose. At least I hope that you realize you're not alone.

Trying Something New

My journey back into the church had its seed in the church-planting initiative that I began in the wake of my leaving. Because I'm so committed to the kingdom and the notion of the church, I could not bring myself to leave until I had a viable alternative. I knew that younger believers were watching my life, so I did not want to walk out on the church and give them reason to do the same. I felt constrained not simply to criticize the church but to be a part of its renewal. I wanted to work from within, but it became increasingly clear to me that I was either not wired to bring reform that way or that people were not wired to receive me. I wanted to be proactive, and I didn't want to be another voice of dissent without actually doing something productive in turn.

After leaving, I spent about two months in personal prayer. My situation was compounded by the fact that there were a number of people (about forty) who were waiting to plant a church with me; word had spread among those closest to me. After my time in prayer, I sensed that we should begin meeting as a group for more prayer. We started Fire by Night, a weekly, two-hour time of intercession (coupled with music) for the city. I felt sure that we needed to spend a season praying as a group for the church in our city and to step away from the role of critics or reformers. This time was very important for us in a number of ways.

While trying to find a place to meet for this unusual prayer meeting, we met a pastor who gave us use of a building that his church owned (an old, converted convenience store). It was perfect for us, and his heart for prayer and his immediate respect and trust started what would be a long-term relationship. This pastor gave us a key to his building, offered us everything he had, and even took notes as we talked with him, asking how the church could change to meet the challenges of the coming generation. I had written about the changes that I saw on the horizon for the church, and he gave those writings to his whole staff to read. We had never been so validated within the church before.

I was floored by this pastor's humility and love for us. Out of that prayer time, which lasted about six months in that form, we forged a partnership with his church. We called ourselves the Underground and eventually became an outreach of that church. I was offered an unpaid position on their staff (missionary in residence) that I accepted. I was also offered a place on the church's teaching team, which I also accepted.

Our approach to church was smaller, but we also saw the value of corporate worship. The Underground was allowed to pursue home-church planting, which was always our vision, while enjoying the traditional Sunday-morning experience. Further we were able to expand our vision for home churches out of this traditional church expression, going on to plant a dozen home churches through this partnership.

Starting Over

I wish I could say that this partnership lasted. We have continued our ministry, encouraging microchurch plants all over our city, but the relationship with the church changed as the leaders changed. Three years and two pastors later, we were right back where we'd started: cut out of a church's mission, disaffected, struggling to stay when we knew it was time to leave.

What is it about the church as we know it that leavers find so difficult? People are leaving, but why? While every situation is different, there are commonalities to our story and those of other leavers, a common critique that unites us.

2

FIVE DEAD FISH
Some of Our Reasons for Leaving

I've spent most of my life on or near a beach. Growing up in Florida has shaped me into a "possibilities" person. Sunshine and oceanfronts are sprinkled through the memories of every phase of my life, and for that I feel blessed.

The beach is a place of life. It stands as a threshold between the vast life of the sea and the life on land. It is also the threshold, it seems, between heaven and earth, a place where the sun touches the land and everything is so alive. I think this is one reason people go to the beach: there we are reminded of God's creative power.

Yet, for us natives, the beach isn't always paradise. Every few years, our beaches are transformed from places of life, family and play to places of death, desertion and decay. The cause: red tide, a wave of toxic water that kills most of the small fish in its path and washes them onto the shores by the thousands.

Recently I drove to one of my favorite beaches, a secluded stretch with no hotels and very few people on the weekdays. I was looking forward to some time of prayer and solitude, but as soon as I stepped out of the car I knew that something was different. As I walked along, I smelled a hint of dead fish, and I could see that the water was calm with inactivity. Yet the beach itself did not betray the effects of red tide. There was the occasional fish head, but not enough to lead me to believe that red tide had again taken its toll.

As I continued to walk along the beach, I noticed tire tracks and grooves cut into the sand parallel to my path along the shore. Finally, I came to a small jetty where the tracks stopped. As I walked out along the jetty, I saw them: thousands of dead fish plowed into a pile. Apparently the dead fish had been removed quickly from the beach by truck. But the truck couldn't get to that spot on the jetty. And that was where the smell was coming from.

Dead fish don't attract tourists; they drive them away. Dead fish are liabilities to the idealized paradise people are seeking. Beach keepers have to plow dead fish away as soon as they possibly can, because death isn't good for business. But it is real.

The church is meant to be a threshold between heaven and earth, between community and mission, between intimacy with God and shared life with each other. But what happens when death is washing up on the shores of our groomed churches? What happens when seeing and worshiping God in the reality of both joy and pain are replaced with neatly packaged messages put to music? Pain is weekly plowed away so that churchgoers can be spiritual tourists. And the voice of dissent is absent: no one will admit that death is near. No one wants to see it.

Listen to these words of one leaver, Crystal, who wrote to me about why she no longer felt church was a place she could stay and grow:

> I think of my parents' church. So much of it plays into the trendiness that appeals to me—to who I long to be in some way. The church is filled with beautiful people. Everyone there looks like they just stepped out of an Abercrombie & Fitch catalog. They are nice looking but still rugged enough to look as if they made a choice to look

that way—just slightly untucked or wearing flip-flops with a dress to show a relaxed, "I don't care" look. The lighting is just right with more beautiful and talented people onstage. They have extreme talent as if they went to a talent pump and filled up and proceeded into the spotlight. Everything goes as planned, the mood, the tone, the relevance. It ends promptly and people return to their lives. It is all so alluring. My family doesn't truly fit in, but when we go, we sit there and the whole time I long to be like these people—long to be in their outfits (matching, mind you) and with their voices and even their spirituality, which seems to be packaged so perfectly. Everyone at this church looks positive—no one appears to be broken. There are ushers at every door, parking attendants at every turn, and I love the experience. I don't go enough to point fingers at this church. They seem sincere in so much of what they do and relevant to the people they want to reach, but something in me is chaffed when I sit there. Something comes up in me that serves me and thinks it is okay to be served because it is what we call church. They are the cutting edge in everything they do, from technology to the musical theater piece they perform, where the singers come out of the congregation dancing to an African American spiritual/Broadway show-tune. They are closer to what people long for . . . or maybe just what I long for. A place to be entertained rather than a place where people go to survive. I don't need survival. I have it on my own. These people too are surviving quite fine outside of the church and here we can be entertained into believing we have just experienced God. I can't say I've had outstanding experiences with God when I've gone there, but I do walk away wowed by the way they think of everyman—who they are trying to reach and the extreme creativity they use to do it. I don't fully understand why it doesn't settle right inside me. I love that they are so artistic and the message so simple, but I get lost in the prettiness of the lure, how it sparkles and shimmers in the light.

There are people in churches who sit as strangers to the manicured life presented onstage. Some have left, in part because they cannot live with that overwhelming sense that something is phony. They are unsure whether it's the people they see or themselves. Someone is lying, and it takes a toll.

We could fill stadiums in every major city with people who have been burned or wounded by bad churches. But you never see them. You never hear them, because the first thing a leaver loses is her voice. In the corners of every city are believers who are no longer visible to churchgoers; they have no platform to speak from, no committee meetings to make their point heard, no friendship with the pastor to get a change made. They are isolated and unorganized. Yet they are an army. In my mind they represent the prophetic hope for the church because they understand perhaps as well or better than anyone what the church needs, where it's failing and what can make it a place of life and joy again.

If we can agree for the moment to face the death of church in the hearts of too many Christians (perhaps even in ourselves), then we can wrestle hope from leaving and possibly discover how we can re-form a more profound vision of what we call church.

Why Leavers Leave

The reasons leavers leave are as varied as the people themselves. Part of what makes this topic difficult to assert with certainty is that leavers aren't connected. They aren't communicating (beyond small personal networks), and they are unorganized. This is a definitional constraint. If they were to organize they would no longer be leavers. However, it's possible to glean some commonalities in leavers and their reasons for leaving. Again, these don't apply to every leaver nor is this an exhaustive list, but it does give voice to some of the concerns that leavers carry with them out the back doors of our churches.

Reason one: Growing out of the message. Everybody loves a convert. When someone comes to Christ in the midst of our community, it's an affirmation of life, of all that we believe, even of the choice we once made. New believers invigorate the mission of the church, reminding each person why the church exists. But what happens when what we call church is two hours on Sunday? And what happens when that time is given almost completely to the needs of the newcomer? Certainly, if someone comes to Christ in a church, the simple salvation message is life for him. It is the beginning of the unfolding of the mystery of God. But what happens to a person after five years who is still hearing a message targeted at the seeker or new believer? What about after ten years, or twenty? Maturity becomes an elusive prospect. Many leavers say so.

They either refer to their leaving as "growing out of" the church or as something more intuitive, that they are inhibiting future growth by staying. Sentiments like this seem to be quite common among leavers: "Evangelicalism helped me to begin with, but I feel I have outgrown it now." Labels are sometimes accurate, and in the case of evangelicalism, it does seem that the bringing of good news and the conversion event hold the greatest prominence in the labor and vision of many churches. It seems they are so fixated on converting seekers or reaching new people that there isn't sufficient thought given about how to reach or be sensitive to the converted. The irony, of course, is that many of these evangelical churches are really seeing very few converts. Don't misunderstand me. The church should reach seekers, but the question is, where should that be done and when should the maturation of the converted take place?

Churches that are being left often make an assumption about the development of believers: that once someone has been a Christian for some years, she need only apply herself to the work of the church; she ceases to have specific and acute spiritual needs of her own. This might suffice if the work of the church is participation in reaching the lost or serving the poor. But too often stage two for a would-be maturing Christian is to serve in the parking lot or to work in the nursery on Sunday morning. Both of these jobs are honorable and valuable, but are they the place of growth, purpose and mission for which believers were created? Further, that prospect of service is still confined to Sunday morning and appears to be unrelated to the daily pressures, challenges and opportunities in the life of the believer.

In his book *The Post-Evangelical,* Dave Tomlinson looks at ideological shifts many leavers make. He argues that "evangelicalism is supremely good at introducing people to faith in Christ, but distinctly unhelpful when it comes to the matter of progressing into a more 'grown up' experience of faith." He maintains that this insensitivity stems from a failure to recognize that spiritual growth is a matter of process; it's a journey. Too often churches have failed to create an experience that serves and nurtures people at each point on that journey.

> *The church has failed us because it really only serves new believers. I'm not sure if that is what they are setting out to do, but everything seems so basic. I don't hear anything more than "Pray and read your Bible," "Be a good witness at work," etc. Very little application beyond that.*
>
> DAVE

James Fowler, a Christian developmental psychologist, in his groundbreaking book *Stages of Faith*, argues that a critical (what he calls Individuative-Reflective) stage is the fourth of six stages toward growth and spiritual maturity. He observes that questions and wrestling with the paradox of certain faith assertions is not only a natural progress from simple adherence but also preferable to it for a number of reasons. Whether you agree with Fowler's ideas or not, they do describe the state that many leavers and other believers find themselves in after years of churchgoing and commitment to God.

Reflecting on Fowler's stages of faith, researcher Alan Jamieson confirms the need that leavers feel for personal maturity. In his book *A Churchless Faith,* he writes, "I have been struck by how almost exclusively these people, on reflection, see their leaving as a moving on, a next step, something they feel drawn to do." This is significant because, while there may be frustration and even anger involved in leaving, behind those emotions lies this admirable motive for growth and development.

Practical theological and church theorist John Drane agrees with the conclusions drawn by William Hendricks in his revealing book *Exit Interviews,* as Hendricks identifies this failure of churches to care for the maturation of their members. Drane laments,

> [Leavers] also frequently claim that leaving the church is actually a way of maintaining their faith. . . . More alarming still is Hendrick's discovery that leaving the church often seems to be a consequence of people dealing with issues of personal maturity and growth in their lives.

Fowler actually argues that a critical phase is part of spiritual growth. People need to be able to ask hard questions about their faith and see that it's real and true, not just for them but for others as well. How can a person going through a critical phase in his spiritual development, questioning the things he had taken for granted, be expected to participate fully in evangelism until he's convinced that what is being said is actually true? Honest inquiry should be a part of any search for truth, and the end result of honest inquiry is not arrogance in having arrived at orthodoxy but confidence both that we can apprehend truth and that it's more complicated than it seems at first glance. Inquiry, then, should lead believers into a deeper awareness of the uncreated God and his covenant love for them. It should also produce the fruit of humility and empower them to be even better evangelists, having wrestled (and continuing to wrestle) with hard questions about faith in Jesus Christ.

The idea of believers being on a journey not only rings true in many leavers' experience but is a profoundly biblical metaphor for discipleship. Jesus calls each of us onto a journey. The simplest metaphor for our life with God is to become a follower, to walk with him. But even that choice is only one step on the journey. The church has to acknowledge the complex stages of growth and adapt itself to include people at each point, not just the first.

Using Jesus' ministry with the disciples as a model for the process of discipleship that we all go through, there are at least three major transitions in the life of a believer, three turning points or lesser conversions. Only the first one saves, but each realization leads to a new level of intimacy and effectiveness. Here Jesus shepherds his followers, leading them differently at each point of maturity. In doing so, he affirms the process or journey of maturation and also acknowledges the complexity of people and their development.

- **Nonfollower to follower.** The operative word here is *come.* It's the call of the disciple, a call to come and follow (see Matthew 4:19; Mark 1:17; Luke 5:27). This is an invitation to anyone who would step onto the journey with Jesus. When

I say *nonfollower,* I mean anyone who isn't an active, growing disciple of Christ. For this person, the ministry goal is surrendering control of his life to Jesus as Lord. True conversion means not simply accepting a propositional truth but choosing to follow Jesus as a result of that belief.

- **Follower to leader.** The operative word here is *go*. It's the call of the apostle or missionary (see Matthew 28:19; John 20:21). Once the person has made the commitment to Jesus as Lord and is living a surrendered life, God calls him deeper, as Jesus did, to go. The first call, "Come, follow me," matures into "Go! I am sending you." Growth for the follower (disciple) comes by "doing likewise" and becoming like Jesus by becoming a leader (apostle). Implicit in the principle of a ministry that multiplies itself is that Jesus calls us to come and follow him so that he can make us "fishers of men." This is necessary not only for the advancement of the gospel and the mission but also for the next step of growth for the disciple.

When I use the word *leader,* I don't necessarily mean someone who is gifted to lead. That is to say, I mean *leader* as something more generic. We are all called to lead, because we follow a leader. To decide that we will not emulate Jesus in one way or another because we aren't "gifted" to do so is to fall short of being a disciple. We lead because he did, just as we proclaim the gospel because and as he did. Some are gifted, and their gift impacts the results. Gifted leaders tend to be able to lead more people with less effort. Those of us who aren't gifted to lead are nevertheless called to lead. It could be as simple as leading our children or family, or leading a neighbor to Jesus. But leadership (influencing others) is part of the journey and the way of Jesus.

- **Leader to world changer.** For those who have accepted the call to leadership, the next call God makes is to become a world changer (see Acts 1:8; 2:47). As the New Testament reveals, this is a job for the Holy Spirit. A follower does what Jesus does—prays, evangelizes, knows the Word, loves others, cares for the hurting—but a leader influences others to do that as well. Jesus left his friends as apostles (sent into the world). Implicit in this transition is the apostles' faithfulness over time to wait on the Spirit and to remain faithful to both their discipleship and apostleship in order to see the world change. The call God makes to our hearts in this transition is one of faithfulness and longevity; we continue not only to be obedient as apostles but also to grow in that calling, leading and *making* more disciples, *building* the kingdom and *multiplying* his work in us. This is the fullness of the Christian ministry, to go, make and teach (according to the Great Commission). World changers are those who remain faithful to their identity as followers of Christ and leaders of others. That is our part. The world, in turn, is changed by the Holy Spirit working in and through us.

If the messages and curriculum of the church are for the initial transition from nonbeliever to believer, those messages will eventually become boring and irrelevant to those who have already made that initial commitment. Turning followers of Jesus Christ and church members into what Jamieson aptly calls "reflective exiles," the church alienates these Christians until they feel they no longer belong to the group that once fed their deepest hunger. All they can do is watch while others find that satisfaction, and they can either relive that experience vicariously through the evangelization of new people or become disaffected with the church and leave to look for personal growth elsewhere.

Many leavers don't abandon what the church stands for or challenge the precepts of evangelicalism itself. Instead they more deeply affirm biblical faith as they look for a truer expression of that faith. Leavers report that the church simply has not helped them navigate the natural process of growth and maturation. They have looked for the next stage for them and found only the perpetual salvation message.

Some leavers feel ashamed that these old songs and old messages no longer move them. Some wonder if something is wrong with them because they are no longer satisfied with simplistic ideas and the basics of the faith. Yet as they stumble upon the Scriptures' exhortation toward maturity, they become restless, gradually growing in confidence that they are, in fact, missing something that was meant to be part of the Christian life, but they are at a loss to know how to get it.

This longing is both healthy and holy. The writer of Hebrews was also dealing with a spiritually immature church that concentrated only on the "foundations" of the faith and seemed content to repeat those teachings to the consternation of the apostle writing to them. His frustration is apparent: "We have much to say about this, but it is hard to explain because you are slow to learn. In fact, though by this time you ought to be teachers, you need someone to teach you the elementary truths of God's word all over again" (Hebrews 5:11-12).

> *The thing that strikes me the most is the manner in which church becomes a routine. Everyone falls in line, follows the order of events in the service: when to greet and say hello, when to pray, sing, shout, etc. I feel like one robot in the midst of others—emotionless, passionless, without zeal.*
>
> JOANN

The writer is being sarcastic, of course. The readers don't need to hear the parochial truths all over again, but they seem to think they do, since that is what they keep hearing. He goes on to insist, "Therefore let us leave the elementary teachings about Christ and go on to maturity, not laying again the foundation of repentance" (Hebrews 6:1).

Leavers are right to be concerned about their maturity. They are right to call into question a church structure that shepherds only the new believer. And it's precisely the phrase "let us leave" that leavers are trying to appropriate. For better or worse, leavers often see leaving the church as leaving basic teaching in search of a deeper revelation of the God they love.

Reason two: Needing to ask questions. So many leavers express that they need to move on because they aren't able to ask the serious questions that deeply disturb their hearts and the simple faith that they have always known. As their faith moves beyond conversion, they begin to ask deeper and more destabilizing questions. Some go through a crisis or loss, finding that clichés about God no longer seem to satisfy. They begin to wonder if there is more. Does the Bible have deeper answers? Does God really hear me? Am I really loved? Are miracles really possible? What really happens when I pray? Who is God really and how can I know? Some of these questions sound like questions that a new believer would ask and some of them are, but the answers that are given the new believer have already been heard, tried and found inadequate.

Some leavers call these answers "Sunday-school answers," a pejorative expression that simply means answers that would be given to a child. People who have known Jesus for years can find these questions troubling, as if their existence weakens the position of Christianity in general and are therefore to be discouraged. However, it's precisely because these are the questions of people who have faith in Jesus Christ that they should not be perceived as a threat but as a search for a more heartfelt and meaningful relationship with God. Questions are helpful for the growth not only of that believer but also of the community.

Discouraging these questions alienates us from the possibility of knowing God in a mature and complex way that is sufficient for the complexities of life. God is not afraid of questions. On the contrary, the word that was planted by his own hand into the hearts of these maturing disciples will be tended by his Spirit and used for the completion of the work that he is doing in them. Questions are a part of the process. As Paul reminds his questioning friends in Philippi, "He who began a good work in you will carry it on to completion until the day of Christ Jesus" (Philippians 1:6).

This longing for a deeper relationship with God and for deeper answers is inspired by God himself, urging believers to go beyond what they have learned, to dig a deeper well and draw from it. This desire should be affirmed, but in many cases it is not. So leavers leave.

Others have questions that aren't related to their own faith in God but to the practice of the church. This was my experience. Some begin to wonder if the way we worship is all there is or if these same sermons or this same liturgy is all there is. There is a natural, healthy curiosity to see how other Christians worship and how they express their devotion and live out their mission. One place that those with questions look is to the New Testament church. There leavers find a church of power and sincere community. This only induces another set of questions. Why isn't our church this way? Is this kind of church possible today? Should we change some of the things we do in order to look more like this beatific vision?

These people, whom Jamieson calls "disillusioned followers," hope for more based on what they believe the church and the Bible has actually taught them. They don't want to abandon their faith or even their church, but they have become disillusioned over the prospect of being heard and seeing change. I put these people in this category because I believe that in both cases they have legitimate questions that, if listened to and considered, could produce either growth and improvement in the church or new awareness in the person asking the question.

In any case, people leave churches because these questions and the process of questioning itself aren't affirmed, and in some cases are discouraged. Since the church is set up to be a spectacle, there are simply no avenues for the average church member to even ask his questions and certainly not to arrive at satisfying answers. There is no formal or informal forum for people to be heard.

Certainly some people still make themselves heard in their churches. But too often even that process is forced or seen as divisive. Often people who make themselves heard have to do so in ways that are seen as (and often are) out of order. The problem is with the process itself. Where and when can everyday members speak into the mission and practice of the church? When can they ask questions together about what they are collectively called to do and offer suggestions on how to do it? Where can they struggle together to ask and answer the lingering questions and doubts they have about God and his people?

Asking questions is a feature of postmodern experience and has to be seen as essential. More and more postmodern people see complexity and uncertainty in life. In the sea of choices and individualized products, questions are infinitely generated and answers are hard to come by. If people don't feel that their questions are valued, they feel undervalued. If there is no place to talk about doubts and questions, does the church seem irrelevant not only in content but also in method? People aren't leaving churches because there is didactic teaching; they are leaving because the didactic teaching has nothing to do with what they are wondering about.

Reason three: Irrelevance. Each of these reasons is related. If there is no value for the maturation of established members, there will be no openness to their questions. There will be no mechanisms in place that allow for doubt and critical dialogue. In turn, the disenfranchised members have no choice but to ignore their questions or to leave to find answers and respect for the process somewhere else.

It follows that the church has become irrelevant and boring because discussions relate only to conversion or initial questions that seekers have, and the questions of maturing believers aren't being addressed. It stands to reason that the church's worship services and other activities would become irrelevant, given those dynamics. It's not irrelevant for all, but just some, and these are the people who will leave.

Again, it should be noted that the church is irrelevant to many more people than just those who leave. People have all kinds of reasons for staying in a church once it has become irrelevant and boring to them, which is one more reason we can thank the leavers for their honesty and boldness, giving others pause to wonder why.

> *It feels a little archaic; it still meets the needs of a 1950s-style church where family is center, the man is the provider of the family, a woman's role is mother and wife. I mean let's face it: most mothers nowadays have a job too; they balance both family and career. Their focus has shifted.*
>
> CRYSTAL

The questions leavers have don't need to be about the church or matters of ultimate concern to become reasons to leave. In some cases, the questions not being answered are also not being asked. People may have a deeper underlying question that may never come to the surface: What does this have to do with my real life? Does what is being said and taught and lived here in the church have anything to do with the life I lead, the family I'm a part of or the job I do? These are the deeper questions of relevance.

In his amazing book *Changing World, Changing Church,*

Michael Moynagh cites, among other changes resulting from the rise of technology, that more employment opportunities will be challenging and fulfilling, leaving monotonous tasks to automation. This means that people will be looking for and finding meaning and satisfaction more and more from their work. Moynagh's challenge about the future may reveal the impact of an irrelevant church experience, especially when related to work:

> As more people seek self-expression through work, the church's absence from the workplace will prove a growing missionary scandal. A crucial sphere of meaning, camaraderie and fulfillment, a sphere of growing significance to ever more people, will be outside the church's orbit.

And maybe it already is. He goes on to ask, "If church is not involved in what really matters to people, why should they take any notice?"

Further, leaders of churches (the mouthpieces, at least) often have no experience in the secular workplace. This is a disadvantage that isn't their fault. Many pastors have sensed a call to ministry and obeyed it. However, a teacher in the church who does not live where his people live may become irrelevant. All of his illustrations will be about the machinations and workings of church. And rightly so, because that is where all his experiences come from. However, these aren't the everyday experiences of most of those listening. Too many sermons are about how to come out of the world and the workplace to worship and serve, but these concepts seem to find their fruition only in or around the church building. This may be because the life of the one who leads revolves around that location. But the questions that people want answered have more to do with how to worship in the marketplace and how to serve inside our homes, on our streets and at PTA meetings.

Again, if people's root questions aren't listened to, there can only be a coincidental success in meeting their deepest needs. For many churches, simply teaching the Bible is enough, and for many people that does seem to be enough. Yet it also seems that, for many others, how those propositional truths and their spiritual meaning are translated into everyday life isn't clear.

The irony, of course, is that those with the answers to the questions are the ones looking for answers themselves. If a church's leader would listen to the questions, doubts and concerns of the people, not only would he communicate value for the questioning process and the people asking the questions, but he would also provide biblical application for the concerns people really have.

Reason four: Nothing meaningful to do. The missing mission of the church has crippled it from the inside out (we will talk about this more later). Not only does the modern church seem to be ineffective at mobilizing its people to do anything in mission, but it also has created systems that tie up its people in nonmission-related activities. I'm convinced that many leavers would not articulate lack of mission as a reason for leaving, but in almost all cases it was a factor. They didn't know it was a factor because it was completely missing. The absence of mission is inconspicuous; people only notice it later, when they've joined a community where it's present.

People were made to contribute, to add value and to see themselves as participants in the purposes of God in the world. Without something meaningful to do, all of the other concerns of life become overwhelming.

I have a friend who was fed up with his church. He could not wait to leave. Yet he was struggling over his motivations for going, and the feeling that he did not belong was mounting. Once I was convinced that his concern was genuine and fair, I planned to encourage him toward some ideas that might connect him with a Christian community he could relate to. Before our meeting, however, he was invited to take a position at the church (something that was, for him, totally unexpected). This changed everything. His outlook shifted and he was willing to live with the limitations of this church because he now believed two things. First, that his voice would be heard. As a member of the staff, he would be able to affect change in the church. Second, that his life mattered in relationship to that church. Until he knew who he was in relation to them, what role he played and how he was going to be able to fulfill his God-given identity in that place, there was no chance of him staying.

People need purpose. But not everyone can take a paid position in a church. Here is the dilemma. Because the mission of the church is the same as that of Jesus—to seek and save the lost, to make disciples of all nations—how does a church ever move on from seeking the lost to making disciples? Obviously they are not mutually exclusive; churches should be able to seek the lost while at the same time affording some concern for the growth, development and discipleship of believers. The problem isn't that churches are remaining concerned about evangelism while they should be moving on to discipleship; it is that only some do the work of the evangelist, which is a major component of discipleship.

It's the genius of God that he would call for an action from believers that simultaneously draws them into a deeper and more meaningful relationship with him and reaches the lost world that he loves. It is participation in the mission that is the bridge between loving sinners and loving saints. Both needs are met in the nexus of mission. Wherever there is meaningful mission and wherever Christians are involved in serving or leading or reaching someone else, they are afforded a place for new and fresh dependence on God as well as a taste of change, through their significant contribution.

Those who participate in the *missio Dei* (God's mission) share in its fruit. Delegating that mission to a few for the rest to watch is only going to produce bored believers. Left to contemplate their own boredom, it seems clear that these believers will begin to wonder why the church is no longer a significant voice in their lives and why it doesn't offer meaningful experiences anymore. Getting believers involved in mission alone may not be enough to keep people from becoming disaffected (given the other concerns mentioned), yet it could go a long way in helping leavers find new kinds of church that awaken their love for God and faith in his kingdom. This is where the church-planting enterprise can offer an open door for leavers to walk back into the church. But more on that later.

Reason five: Using money. Most Christians live with some degree of dissonance about money and the church. Some are pragmatic, resolving that it simply takes money to do anything, and therefore we need to raise money for the church. Others spiritualize the process, asserting that the money does not really go to buildings, programs and staff salaries but to God. Others talk about the church being the storehouse referred to in Malachi.

Perhaps the most uniformly accepted doctrine of the church is that of the tithe. Maybe that's because it's so clearly spelled out in Scripture, or maybe it's the one doctrine that is necessary to keep the church running. Giving is undeniably taught in Scripture, but the theological gymnastics that are done with the Bible when it comes to money is truly uncanny. Leavers often decry these practices. Many will live with a degree of discomfort about money, choosing to keep their concerns silent until something else triggers that last-straw event and the money problem is simply "another thing" that they point to for leaving. Some leavers (like me) leave because of what is taught and practiced in regard to money.

It can be confusing to say that the money we give on a Sunday morning is going to God, when it really just looks like it's going to maintain the services that the church provides, mostly for me and my family. Leavers wonder, If I'm the one who benefits from the gift, is that really giving? It is like the man who buys his wife a power tool for Christmas. He can wrap it and label it as a gift for her, but if he's the one who benefits from it, isn't it a gift for him? Also troublesome is the relatively new contention by pulpiteers that if you give into this particular offering or toward this ministry (which often means into their own pockets), God will "bless" you with a hundred times more money.

Setting aside the question of authenticity for a moment, is giving in hopes of a return really giving? If I put ten dollars into something that I believe will result in a thousand-dollar return, that is not giving; it's an investment (and a very good one at that). Even if the Bible makes that promise, which I don't believe it does, how can we say that such a transaction is actually giving or an expression of love? "This is how we know what love is," John wrote, "that Jesus Christ laid down his life for us" (1 John 3:16). Giving is paying a price without hoping to get anything in return. It was Jesus who first taught us about altruism, after all.

It's hard to stomach how far some have strayed from the elementary teachings about money and giving. Leavers see this. I think most people do. But they quiet their objections because they don't want to be seen as contentious, stingy or faithless. I'm not referring to blatant misuse of money by church leaders here. It isn't the exceptions that we need to consider here but rather the rule. While some church leaders are thieves, and droves of people will leave churches because of them, most churches and church leaders struggle with more pedestrian problems. They wrestle with the problem of taking money given to God for the work of God and stewarding that money in a way that reflects the biblical concern for the Great Commission and the poor. This is such a difficult task for the contemporary North American church that it has become a kind of crucible. If a church has character weaknesses or integrity flaws, they will surface in this area. Money has a way of having its way. It also has a way of taking the place of God.

Jesus knew that money is one of God's chief rivals for the devotion of the human heart, and he graciously delineated for us that it comes down to choosing one or the other; the two could not coexist as driving forces in the human heart—nor, for that matter, in the heart of a church. For that reason, money tends to reflect the values of a group (and individuals too). Jesus said that where your treasure is, your heart will be. If you want to see where your heart is, take a good look at the entries in your checkbook.

This is true for churches also. If you look at where the bulk of money is spent, you will find one of the reasons leavers leave. When the leaver lacks character, she will leave because she thinks not enough money is being given to programs that benefit her. But leavers who ask why money isn't going to feed the poor, to serve those in prison or to bring the gospel to those that have not heard are raising valid questions. Those of us who have left churches simply because money was not given where we wanted it or into programs that served us ought to repent.

Lack of clarity, integrity and a clear biblical mandate on how to spend money in God's name have all contributed to a precarious relationship between the church and its resources. Since abuses and excesses in this area are many, money has also become a reason why believers are leaving.

One Reason Not to Leave: The Use of Absolute Terms

While studying the phenomenon of leaving, I also uncovered that people, particularly young people, are leaving the church because of its use of absolute terms. In his book *The Post-*

Evangelical, Tomlinson argues that the increasing disillusionment of postmoderns with the church has to do with propositional truth; since a scientific view of reality is no longer palatable, spiritual truths mediated by the church should no longer be couched in scientific terms, such as facts. In agreement with Lutheran theologian Walter Brueggemann, he writes,

> Reality is no longer the fixed arrangement of the scientific era. . . . This is actually a considerably more hospitable situation to spiritual and theological possibilities. But such possibilities cannot be put forward in absolute terms. We can take a full part in negotiating the future of our culture, provided we neither pretend to be "privileged insiders"—people who know the truth with certainty—nor allow ourselves to be "trivialized outsiders."

I have three problems with this line of thinking. First, it seems by definition that "reality" is what it is and will always be nothing more than it is. It was never fixed for all to see, even if science said it was (which it did not; science is actually a matter of probability). Postmodernity has not erased the revelations of Newtonian physics.

Second, postmodernity may be more favorable to spiritual possibilities, but this is not, in fact, what the gospel is. The gospel is actually a proclamation of the revelation of God in the person of Jesus Christ—not the abstracted Christ, but the actual historical figure who can be known through the preserved account of his life in the canon of Scripture and a living relationship with his Spirit. In the endless unknowing of postmodernity, people are actually looking for something quite different—something certain, something secure.

Third, Tomlinson falls into a common postmodern contradiction: he argues against absolute terms using absolute terms. Absolute terms still have value in the free market of ideas; even postmoderns like Tomlinson can't persuade or

teach without them. Being a postmodern myself, I'd nevertheless argue that while absolute terms need to be used sparingly,
they are actually the key to our success in ministry. People are,
more than ever, looking for answers.

As to Christians being "privileged insiders," that is simply
the case, given that the gospel is a proclamation of the revelation of God. But how we use or display our privileged insights
is more important than ever. Humility, dialogue and honesty
about our struggles is critical in bringing the gospel to postmoderns, but when I look at the evangelism of Paul, Peter,
Stephen or Philip, I see a deep belief that they had come to
know the living God through Jesus Christ, and their terms
were anything but uncertain.

If I can't say with total confidence to someone else "Jesus
loves you," then Christian mission is impossible. The earliest
Christian creed was an assertion of absolute truth (albeit limited). In the *Recovery of Mission,* Vinoth Ramachandra puts it
this way:

> The earliest Christian profession "Jesus is Lord" was
> never merely a statement of personal devotion but a
> claim to universal validity. Christian mission made sense
> only on the premise that the crucified Jesus had been en-
> throned as the true Lord over the whole world.

Eddie Gibbs argues that we do have to change the way we
talk about truth to use more narrative, while remembering the
transcendent reality of the overarching story of God and its su-
premacy in all the "spiritual possibilities" we consider. In a section of his book *ChurchNext,* "From Propositional Truth to Dialogue and Story," Gibbs writes,

> The task facing the church is not to attempt to remake the
> story . . . but too see beyond the story to the good news of
> the breaking into history of God's kingdom. It is that re-

ality that passes judgment on every human story, whether national myths or personal journeys through life.

To say that we aren't insiders as coheirs with Christ would actually be dishonest, and postmoderns want honesty. Churches have to be confident in the immutable character of Christ and the irreversible work that he did for us on the cross, while at the same time being confident that we are fallible and weak but bearers of this truth nonetheless.

In my ministry with college students, we've had to talk less about apologetics and tell more stories, but still people are hungrier than ever to hear someone tell them something that is true. I think what has changed is that they may not believe our absolute statements if they don't see it in human form. Incarnation of the truth is more important than ever. Proposition alone isn't enough to convince the postmoderns I've worked with; you can make an absolute claim, but it also has to be embodied in what that person sees. It's the blending of truth and love that makes for the best witness to postmoderns. For this reason, I'm reluctant to include the use of absolute terms as a reason why people leave churches. I think there is still a place (albeit diminished) in the church of postmoderns for absolute terms.

Am I Right to Feel This Way?

For those who are reading this and find themselves wondering if they have done something wrong by leaving or wanting to leave, take heart. Again, you're not alone, and if the concerns you have about your church are born from your love for them and from your understanding of Scripture then, yes, you're right to feel this way. If you have already left, the question now is, what to do? Keep reading. The beach was meant to be a place of life, beauty, rest and the creative power of God. Don't abandon it yet.

3

OUR SCANDALOUS CHOICE
Wondering How to Leave

*C*alling something "church" does not make it holy. While attending a small church in Middle America, my close friend Beth (not her real name) was often asked to baby-sit. One such job was for the seven-year-old son of a deacon and divorcee. Beth was thirteen at the time and became this man's only baby-sitter. He often asked her to stay the night, even after he had come home. Over time he convinced Beth that he was in love with her and took advantage of her in every way.

Everyone in the church ignored the situation. After all, this man was a leader and one of the biggest givers to the small and struggling church. Once the truth of the abuse Beth had suffered began to surface, the pastor called her a liar (although she had never been known to lie) and assumed she was making it up. In spite of the law that requires pastors to report abuse allegations, he chose to keep it to himself, never even asking the man in question about it.

Beth's parents were outraged, complaining to the pastor and insisting that he side with the little girl. He responded by excommunicating them from the church, even posting a sign outside the door of the church saying that their family was not welcome because they were ungracious and sowing seeds of discord.

Thankfully, the district attorney was not so quick to ignore what was an overwhelming amount of evidence corroborating all that Beth had said. Three years later, a jury would also agree and find the man guilty on fifty-one counts of sexual misconduct against a minor. Even on the stand, when called as witnesses, both the pastor and his wife stood by their biggest supporter, contending that they had done nothing wrong.

There are two scandals here: the predator's actions and the church all but sanctioning them. I tell you that story to assert a simple yet important truth: some churches are bad and should be left. I'm not saying that every church is bad or that you should leave yours. I'm simply acknowledging that there are times when a committed believer needs to get off a sinking ship. Admittedly, this is an extreme example, but experiences like Beth's are far too common.

By outlining the extreme, we demystify the organization we call church. While ideologically it's a collection of people like no other, full of divine potential and kingdom destiny, in practice, in the stark reality of what we call church—a building with a steeple and pastors and Sunday-morning worship services—it's no different from any other human organization. Most organizations would not abide this kind of abuse. But it does happen, along with everything in-between. Perhaps what Beth's story illustrates most clearly is something that most leavers know: churches, like everything else, are flawed. We should not leave them just because we see a flaw nor should we be blindly loyal to them simply because they have adopted the moniker "church." There are good churches and there are bad churches. There are churches that need to be left because the best thing—for the kingdom and for the communities where they wield the name of Jesus—would be for them to be people-less.

It's remarkable just how easy it is to become a church and, once existing as a church, just how easy it is to continue. Just because there's a sign in the front of the building that says "Church" doesn't mean that it is church. It's okay to admit that some churches don't deserve the name, and that opens the door to discussion.

Negative Spiritual Consequences of Staying

Nobel Prize winner and Holocaust survivor Elie Wiesel wrote an amazing little play called *The Trial of God*. It's a reenactment of a real event that he witnessed as a boy in a German death camp. Wrestling with the profound injustice being played out before their eyes, Jews in this particular camp had to deal with the theological implications of being both "chosen" by God and apparently abandoned. The reality of the situation is that they had charges against God, and like Abraham, they wanted to ask God, "Will not the judge of all the earth do right?" (Genesis 18:25). So, the educated and most religious men of the community set up a court to try God and to hear arguments for and against him and then to pass a judgment of their own. Wiesel was only a boy but remembers parts of the trial. After hours of testimony and deliberation, the rabbis found God guilty of crimes against his people. With breathtaking irony, they noted to each other that it was time for prayers, and all adjourned.

The story illustrates that religion can be as much about culture and identity as it is about personal conviction, faith or relationship with God. The rabbis had decided God was not just and had, in fact, wronged them, but they held on to their religious tradition because it was theirs. Although they may have no longer loved God, they continued their traditions anyway.

We can continue with church because it has become who we are. We can find identity and comfort in defining our lives in religious terms. Too many churchgoers have long since abandoned the idea that church can offer a life-giving encounter with God. For many, the seemingly pointless monotony of church attendance has made them callous toward God. They even decide that God is not really for them. And yet they keep coming. I think this phenomenon is tantamount to spiritual catastrophe. Ritual and tradition can support and even inspire faith, but it can never replace it. Staying connected to a ritual that no longer affords a real connection with God is not only unproductive, it's spiritually dangerous.

No one was ever so kind and understanding of sinners (of every variety) as Jesus Christ. In the face of almost every sin, he was simply unfazed. Yet anger and occasionally violence were his reactions to the sin of hypocrisy. He simply could not stomach it. In the end, I believe that Jesus was so hard on this particular sin because it's more dangerous, more insidious to religious life than any other. It's the sin that blinds us to repentance and creates disembodied beliefs and self-delusion. It separates a person from reality; you can say one thing and do another. It's more than a loss of integrity; it's a loss of truth, of reality.

Continuing to attend a religious service or event after you have long since decided that event or program actually keeps you from authentic encounter with God is hypocrisy. It isn't good for you, it isn't good for the kingdom, and it isn't even good for that church. Churches filled with people who no longer believe in that church and no longer engage faith to be there become hollow, heartless museums, rehearsing the liturgy of

> *I'm not sure when it started, but I think a lot of it was after reading about these exciting places where God was really moving. I longed for that—for relationships to be built that would impact the kingdom, whether with Christians or non-Christians. But every Sunday was the same old thing. I could sit there for ninety minutes and not really have any contact with anyone.*
>
> DAVE

words and actions that once held life for some who now are only acting.

There are times when church is dry, when reading the Bible is dry. I'm not offering license to abandon discipline every time you don't feel excited or full of faith when practicing it. Gathering for worship can be just such a discipline that we maintain in spite of our spiritual melancholy. Yet if you don't believe that reading the Bible in a particular way or gathering for worship in a particular way is helping you to encounter God (because it has been years since you experienced it), then by all means stop doing it in that particular way. But don't stop pursuing, worshiping and loving God. Rather, change what you're doing so that those spiritual disciplines remain.

Some years ago, I always studied the Bible through detailed analysis of one manuscript at a time. That meant deep reflection on the meaning of short phrases and even words in the context of a short passage, story or episode. For years that approach was life-giving. Not every time, but more often than not I learned, and more important, I sensed God teaching and speaking to me. That is why we open our hearts to the Word of God, because Jesus is the Word and to hear him is life.

But after many years of doing Bible study in the same way, I found myself less enthusiastic about it. Without really noticing, I stopped doing it. Being in ministry, I would still study the Bible to prepare for messages or teaching assignments, but very rarely on my own and from my heart. I finally realized that I had lost motivation. At first, I questioned my own spiritual validity, thinking there must be something wrong with me. *I don't want to study the Bible? How bad is that?* But feeling guilty did not make the times of study feel like less of a chore. Then I tried to get creative. Instead of reading the Bible the way I always had, I decided to read larger portions, skimming the stories, seeing how they connected together in the larger context.

One night two friends and I tried to skim the whole Bible to discover how each book primarily depicted God. It was like that famous painting by Salvador Dali, "Gala Contemplating the Mediterranean." When you look very closely, you see the detail and the wonder of a hundred tiny paintings, but when you step back, there is a whole painting to admire. That time of Bible reading was rejuvenating.

Ignatius had the great idea of trying to imagine yourself as a player in the biblical narrative you're reading. Praying the Scriptures, singing them, listening to the Bible on CD—all of these have helped me to remain committed to an encounter with the Word of God himself and not simple "Bible study" as I had narrowly defined it.

Our commitment to God is often mediated by behaviors and spiritual practices, but these practices are not God. They aren't what we are committed to. Our commitment to God, his people and his mission has to supersede the methods related to those things. In truth, that is what church really is.

Can You Really Leave the Church?

What is church? Most believers would agree that it isn't the building or the programs but something more. In practice, that theory is rarely tested. What makes a church a church? Is it music? A sanctuary? A pastor? A weekly religious gathering? Discovering exactly what makes something church will help us determine what we must stay committed to and what is acceptable to consider abandoning in the pursuit of God. I'm sure that we should remain committed to the church, as the body of Christ, its head and the mission that it has been given, but so much of what we call "church" simply isn't. Making that delineation is necessary before we can talk about where to leave and where to stay.

How we think about church is important when defining it. On the one hand, we can tend to think of church practically as a condition, that is, as something concrete that can be defined. When we think about church or examine the use of the word in daily life, we can see that we do tend to understand church as a condition, or a concrete concept. For instance, we ask a friend, "Will I see you at church this weekend?" or "Have you visited that church on Third Street?" Generally what we mean when we use the term this way is a building, a weekly service or a group of programs attended by a group of people (albeit a somewhat transient group).

However, when the discussion turns theological or theoretical, we understand church to be more of an ideal. We are the church, people understand. There is such a thing as the invisible church, of which we are all somehow a part. The truth is, the church is both an ideal and a condition, but not always in the way we conceive it.

Marriage is a similar concept. On the one hand, marriage is a condition based on a vow and contract that was either made or not made. On the other hand, marriage is an ideal that can be measured as a continuum moving two disconnected people (who are married but don't act like it) to a state of profound partnership, love and unity. If we think about marriage only as an ideal, we can never think of ourselves as truly married. This could be problematic. If one spouse says to the other, "We barely even talk anymore; this is not a marriage," is the couple not married? Does that appraisal give each partner license to look for another? Of course not, because the ideal is mediated by the condition. A couple may be far from the ideal of marriage, but they are still fulfilling the condition of marriage.

Likewise, all churches fall short of the ideal of church. That is to say, every church can still grow at least a little into more of what it could mean to be the church. You don't leave a church simply because it isn't living up to an idealized definition. However, the conditional definition of the church should never be an address or a worship service or a pastor. The issue is that, unlike marriage, we have not clearly defined the condition. Often we have thought of the condition as self-defining. In other words, if someone says they are a church, then they must be.

You may have heard someone say, "No church is perfect." And that is true. What she means is that finding an imperfection is a silly reason to leave, because you're destined to find imperfections everywhere. I completely agree. What I'm interested in helping us to determine is this: does this organization, service or group meet the simple biblical criteria for being a church? We need an ecclesial minimum that helps us make a concrete definition of church that's not bound by era or culture or doctrinal differences. Once we are part of a true church, we can commit to one another and work toward the ideal.

Certainly church is more than a condition, but it is not less. Just talking about the church as an ideal isn't helpful when the dissonance we feel from being there is so great. What is it about our church experience that is so wrong? The internal conflict we feel stems from not having an established ecclesiology. The difference between complaining and prophetic leaving can be very slight, and that difference is mostly about knowing what the church has to be. What we really need is a conditional ideal. That is to say, church has to be at least something.

4

OUR BUILDING PROJECT
The Leavers' Reconstruction of Church

*M*y third child, seven-year-old Eve, is wonderfully eccentric and strangely insightful when it comes to spiritual things. Each time I'm alone with one of my kids, I try to ask how his or her relationship with God is going. I want to empower my children to think about interacting with God as their true Father and not just performing religious duties to please me or their mother. One night I was out with Eve and asked her that question. She responded with her usual flare, "Wonderful."

I was a little surprised, so I asked, "How do you know your relationship with Jesus is going so well? How can you be so sure?"

She replied, "Because he calls my name at night."

Being church is about being known by God. How does he define us? Just as some individuals will be surprised on the day of reckoning to find out that Jesus does not know them (even though they had called him Lord), I also think that some churches would be surprised to know that God does not know them as churches. That is not to say that God does not know that people gather at that building on that day, or whatever they do; he knows everything. Rather it is to say that God does not know them as a church, as a group of his people. What makes church real, known by God, has to be what motivates us once we have left the counterfeits.

Ecclesial Minimum

Acts 9 tells the story of the conversion of a religious zealot named Saul. He was particularly annoyed at the new sect of Judaism called the Way, and he spearheaded a wave of persecution against those who would later be called Christians. All that changed the day he had a blinding vision of the resurrected Jesus calling him to worship, community and mission.

He was being called into the church. These three things are what Jesus calls all of his people into, and they are the three essential elements of what it means to be church.

Worship. Like the calling of the other disciples, the initial confrontation Saul had with Jesus required obedience and sacrifice. No simple intellectual ascent was being solicited. Jesus wasn't asking Saul to pray the sinner's prayer or to believe on his name. He was commanding him. As at the calling of the fishermen in Galilee, Jesus was giving only two options: drop everything and follow me, or don't. Saul chose to obey.

At the heart of that choice is both the identity of Jesus (as Lord) and the identity of his disciples (as followers). This is worship, both to understand the object of our worship as being infinitely worthy of any sacrifice (no price too great) and to understand ourselves as subservient and obedient to that object. Perhaps reflecting on this event, Saul (who became known as Paul) would later write, "I urge you, brothers, in view of God's mercy, to offer your bodies as living sacrifices, holy and pleasing to God—this is your spiritual act of worship" (Romans 12:1). Saul understood immediately that to follow meant that Jesus would lead and he would follow.

Further, following would come at a great price, because worship is about love and love is about sacrifice. The first thing Saul was shown was "how much he must suffer for [Jesus'] sake" (Acts 9:16). Believing in Jesus is good, but there is a deeper kind of commitment that is the cornerstone of saving faith. Following Jesus means he is the leader and he is

Lord. Church has to embody, embrace and imbibe that reality. This is the first element of the minimum for church: the worship and acknowledgment of the one true God and his incarnation Jesus Christ. I don't mean worship in the sense that we commonly understand it, as a time of thinking about God and his worth, but rather the offering of one's life to God in total surrender in proportion to the revelation of his worth. This is worship.

Part of what it means to be church is to be submitted to God and Jesus as Lord. When a group of people is known by God in this way, they are one step closer to being the church. It's impossible to think of a collection of people as the church without Jesus Christ as the head. We are his body, and our worship (submission to him) makes that real.

In my sophomore year, my brother got into some trouble. People cut into him and when I defended him, I was called naive. He wasn't shunned by everyone, but the ones who did were the ones with power. I think more than hurting me, it scared me. What was to keep me from being outcast in the same way?

KIM

Community. The first lesson this story teaches is that Jesus deeply identified with his people. Saul was threatening the disciples and the people of God, yet Jesus seemed unwilling to delineate. "I am Jesus," he said, "whom you are persecuting" (Acts 9:6). There is a very real relationship between disciples of Jesus and Jesus himself, one that's so profound that God does not separate them in his mind. When beholding the true church, the people of God, he says to himself, *That is my body,* just as you might say when looking down at your torso, arms, hands, legs and feet. To know Jesus, to enter into a relationship with him, means to become a part of his body.

Church isn't church if it's not done in community. There is no such thing as a church of one. God saves individuals, but he very clearly brings them into relationship with each other. Part of what it means to accept the gospel of reconciliation is to be reconciled with God and the other part is to be reconciled with each other.

The New Testament often pictures the bride of Christ not as an individual but as a collective. What makes us the bride of Christ is that we are something together that we are not alone. For this reason, church, if it is to be fully church, must involve some level of community, people relating to other believers in light of the other components: worship and mission. You can have a group of people who worship together but never really interact. That's fine. In fact, it can be a very powerful and beautiful experience, one that enriches everyone involved and brings glory to God. But it's not church. It's worship. Likewise you can have people gathering in community, like a sitcom cast or a sports team. Those relationships can be very real, rich and meaningful, but they're not church.

That is why, immediately after Saul's vision, God called him into relationship with other believers—a relationship that would take some getting used to for people like Ananias. Even though he was a scary addition to the family, Saul was nevertheless necessarily drawn immediately into the family of God and into community. This was hard for Ananias, but this is what the church is supposed to be all about; this is why the church is the opposite of the world that Saul lived in. This is one way that the church can stand as a contrast to the unforgiving, homogeneous, convenience-based social enclaves where Westerns align themselves. Too many of us convert to Christ and find a new kind of loneliness and superficiality with a spiritual face. It was not enough for Saul to have a vision of Jesus, repentance and dedication to a call to suffer and serve. The man who would become Paul was truly changed in this regard: Saul was a loner, alienating and alienated, but Paul would write.

To the Philippians, he wrote, "It is right for me to feel this way about all of you, since I have you in my heart; for whether I'm in chains or defending and confirming the gospel, all of you share in God's grace with me. God can testify how I long for all of you with the affection of Christ Jesus" (Philippians 1:7-8).

To the Romans, he wrote, "How constantly I remember you in my prayers at all times; and I pray that now at last by God's will the way may be opened for me to come to you. I long to see you so that I may impart to you some spiritual gift to make you strong" (Romans 1:9-11).

All over the known world he had friends whom he loved and who loved him, because he'd had an encounter with Jesus, and Jesus forever changed the way ministry—and life, for that matter—was meant to be done. If the perfect man, Jesus, set up his life in a small community of friends, shouldn't we? After all, he didn't need it. But he knew it was better—life, success, fruit, joy, sadness, laughter, failure is all a little better when done in the company of friends.

The other day I saw my youngest son, Simeon, sitting in his highchair, eating from a bowl of cereal. Only two, he's typically a bit reckless with his food, so I wondered about the wisdom of giving him cereal with milk in a bowl and leaving the rest to chance. I watched for a while. He wasn't very interested in actually eating it but began to spin his bowl. The cereal and the milk spun wildly out. It actually looked like fun, so I kept watching. By the time he had finished, almost no cereal was inside that bowl. Some pieces were on the floor, some on the table, some in the seat of the highchair (which the dog was reaching up to eat) and some even in his hair.

I learned something from his display—a lesson in physics. Relationships bond the church, keeping it together through the struggles of faith and mission. The force exerted on a group of people when they're together can be extraordinary. Having lived in an intentional community with eight other adults for the past ten years, I can attest that just living together generates conflict and pressure. Yet that same pressure, whether it's interpersonal or external, bonds us, locking us together in a way that mere interaction can't. Like glue, shared experience—especially in difficult experiences—holds the church together.

Think of the concepts of centrifugal and centripetal force. When a mass is bonded together, like a top, and then spun on its axis, the force created by the spinning actually helps to keep the motion going. The bond between the elements serves to increase the force of the spinning, both stabilizing what is being spun and helping to keep it going. This is called centripetal force. Conversely, when the elements of a whole are not bonded together, like a bowl of cereal, the centrifugal force of spinning actually throws the pieces outward, away from each other, toward chaos. Simeon spinning the bowl created centrifugal force.

People leave churches in part because the force of life on a church without deep community is centrifugal. Any pressure, disagreement, conflict or philosophical difference can end in "divorce" because the bond isn't there. We have to build churches where people can really know each other, where they can be connected in a deeper way than a loose commitment to a certain style of music or a pastor. These are fine things for creating common ground, but they hardly act as glue. Too many churches resemble country clubs or malls, where people gather as an enclave, sharing certain things in common, such as an interest in golf or boating or shopping. But what they share isn't about them. That is to say, what they share is an interest in something other than each other. They are in the same place, perhaps even doing the same things, because they have something in common, but that commonality is not organic and it is not human. For that reason, the humanity in a mall is subservient to the common goal of shopping. If someone shuts down the stores I like or makes a scene or plays music too loud, I will simply find another mall. Christian community, an essential element of church, is intended to be so much more.

Here is the irony of community: you as an individual will never reach your personal destiny, fulfill who you are, use your gifts effectively or unlock your potential until you're in community. The personal and the communal are inextricably bound, because God is found in his body. In community you depend on, are challenged by and receive from God in a way you can't anywhere else. It's an avenue of grace for us; don't block that avenue by failing to pursue community.

By the way, I think we don't pursue community (although our very souls long for it) because we have been brainwashed to think too individualistically.

Mission. Saul's story is a story of conversion, of turning from one way of life to another (see Acts 9). It's one of the biggest swings or redemptions in the Bible. It isn't a story about commitment to God; Saul was very committed to God, but that commitment was misguided and he was lost. As a leader he was willing to sacrifice everything for what he believed. This did not change when he met Jesus on the Damascus road. What changed was his view of God's heart and his mission in the world. And this is the key to the final element that God called Saul into and that makes us church: mission.

Saul was already in mission; it was just the wrong one. The Holy Spirit works in every human being to see him become a believer, to help him to put faith in Jesus Christ. Subsequently the Spirit's work is to see every believer make a total commitment, to become a worshiper, for every worshiper to find and gather into meaningful community, to be redeemed from the idolatry of individualism and to go together (as Jesus sent people) into the mission of building the kingdom of God. The end result is everyone participating in the mission of God. It is the church in the battle, flexing its muscles and using its strength, love, sacrifice, suffering, courage, hope . . .

Finally, church is church only if it engages in the mission of God. Just as we were called and created to worship and for community, we were created for mission. God gives gifts to his church to equip it to accomplish the commission of making disciples. This is our reason for existing. God's heart is for the expansion of his kingdom and the increase of his glory. That means that those of us who worship God, recognizing his true nature and in turn glorifying him, have to testify to the good news of that kingdom, which means to include every human being. Delivering good news to our lost friends by proclamation and demonstration is the core purpose of every worshiper and every community of God. By adding this purpose to our worship and our gatherings, we become church.

Worship, gathering and mission—all three functioning together in any form represent the church of Jesus on earth. Everything else is extra.

- A group of men who meet in a bar after work to talk about living deeper, more surrendered lives in which they take time to pray for their families and invite their nonbelieving friends to share a meal and the gospel would be church.

- A Sunday morning service where a great organ resounds the glory of God and the music and preaching move thousands of unrelated people, who return the next week to have the same experience, never engaging the mission or each other—this is not church.

- A group of mothers invites other mothers to a park after school and builds relationships with them and their kids, hoping to share Jesus with them. They also meet to pray for each other, listen to struggles, cry together and recommit to the goal of living for Jesus and reaching every mother at that school. That is church.

- The church softball team plays in a church league, worships together on Sunday and even enjoys good fellowship before and after the games with Christians from their own team and from other churches. This is not church.

Generally, if you break down why leavers have left or should leave churches, it can come down to one of these three areas: (1) God is not honored, (2) people aren't in community with each other, or (3) they aren't reaching anyone. Leavers will rarely recognize their reasons in these terms. They tend to articulate the reasons mentioned in chapter two. But most reasons originate in a church's deficiency in one of these areas.

There are myriad other reasons people get fed up with church, but I would argue that many of the more petty reasons are related to a breakdown in one of these three, particularly mission. If people are engaged together in meaningful, fruitful mission, they can and will overlook small things. If, however, there is no meaningful mission that a church or its people are engaged in together, the result can be disastrous.

Think of a face. Even the most attractive face becomes flawed given enough scrutiny. In fact, every face, if stared at long enough, becomes less attractive. You will notice a lack of symmetry in the nostrils or earlobes. Perhaps the top lip is slightly out of proportion with the bottom, or you notice a scar or blemish. The point: if you look for flaws, you will find them. Churches, like people, don't hold up well to scrutiny. When we are engaged in more important things, we don't scrutinize; we appreciate the obvious and overlook our church's flaws.

I once counseled a young couple that argued all the time. They often were embarrassed by how petty and silly their arguments seemed when explained to me, though those arguments had been so heavy and important in the heat of the moment. They wanted to have children but reasoned, "We're just too messed up. How can we bring a child into our home when we can't even get along." I disagreed. The truth was that having a child was just what they needed, and time has demonstrated why. Babies need attention. They take whatever time you have. They are also precious and infinitely valuable. They are demanding and worth it at the same time. For this couple, their newborn became a mission they could agree on. Their attention was focused on the baby, not on each other.

At the end of a long day after the baby was put to bed, they had less energy to argue about the petty things that used to monopolize their evenings. They were less aggressive and more understanding toward each other as they began to see themselves as partners in an amazing and significant ministry to this new life. The baby brought the couple new challenges, but they argued a lot less; when they did, the matters tended to matter more.

When we aren't engaged in mission as a community, we tend toward scrutiny, because we have nothing better to do. We scrutinize the pastor, the pastor's wife, the music, the instruments, the Sunday school, the sermon, the parking lot, the paint on the walls, what so and so said about so and so, and the list goes on. When we engage in mission, we tend not to look so carefully at the flaws in our compatriots; we don't have the energy. We focus on the mission itself and its fruit, and when we have conflict, it's only when necessary and only to move the mission forward.

Limiting Church

When happening together, these three components make up the church. As I said before, by this definition, some things we call church are not. And some things we don't call church are. If we depict these three components as concentric circles, we can see that we are capable of doing not just one (or none for that matter), but also combinations of two at a time. For instance, it's possible to worship with people who don't know each other and who do no mission together. Some churches are just warehouses for worshipers. People come in once a week, unconnected and unsent. They return each week to sincerely present themselves to God in worship. This is a wonderful thing. But it is not church.

Likewise, a community of Christians can exist on a softball team, in a classroom or in a neighborhood. People can share their lives in a deep way but never pray or worship together and never participate in mission. This kind of community can be beautiful and deeply encouraging; it's a good thing. But it is not church.

Or a group of people can gather to participate in the mission of God: feeding the homeless once a week, doing street or door-to-door evangelism or building a home for a single mother. This group could be doing a great service and see people won to the kingdom of God. But they aren't relationally connected, not sharing their lives, and they don't submit themselves to God together. This kind of ministry is excellent and can be very effective. But it is not church.

While these three things individually are good, when they're isolated from the others or when our spiritual experience is limited to just one of them, we face particular pitfalls. God has configured the church to be a refuge for us. He has called us into the church because it helps us to live as Jesus lived. Jesus was committed to these three things and little else. He did not have committees or music or buildings or offerings. He wasn't married; he didn't have children; he didn't have a big house or a nice car (or a donkey, for that matter). So none of these things can be a requirement for being a follower or being the church.

Without all three aspects, we can fall into error:

- *Just worship: hypocrisy.* If our spiritual life is confined to a privatized worship that's sincere but doesn't lead us into mission or into deep relationships with others, we face the threat of hypocrisy. We offer ourselves to God but don't put into practice what his presence and his Word would require.

- *Just community. idolatry.* If we pursue deep relationships but fail to live those relationships in the light of the mission of God or to submit those relationships to the headship of Jesus, we risk idolatry. Deep relationships unmediated by a concern for the kingdom and mission of God will take over our hearts, taking a place that should belong only to God. These unbalanced relationships will quickly become unhealthy and detrimental to our spiritual life.

- *Just mission: pride.* If our spiritual life is confined to independently pursuing mission but not open, accountable friendships or dependence on God, we risk becoming our own God. Taking the mission on ourselves without realizing our need for God or the people of God will certainly lead to error and egomania.

Combining two of the three gets us closer to being church, but because each of these three is a minimum, our life together is not church unless it embodies all three. Some churches are places of *worship and community.* People know and love each other and present themselves to God in worship every week together. Most of what we call church looks like this. But if mission isn't part of what is happening, no amount of pomp and circumstance, rituals or sacraments can make it church. Churches that are nonmissional can become trivial, self-focused and hypercritical. Churches that lack engagement in mission emphasize programs for believers, and growth is possible only as Christians transfer in from other churches.

Parachurch organizations, mission agencies and city ministries often focus on *worship and mission*. A megachurch also can encourage participation in worship together and occasionally in mission ventures to the city or the world, but the people often remain unconnected and unknown to each other. This overlap can be effective for the kingdom, but the absence of community keeps it from being sustainable, because the people are susceptible to burnout and high turnover rates. Mission without community is painstaking and tedious.

Secular mission agencies focus on *community and mission*. They may be in community with each other as they pursue a mission, but without a corporate commitment to Jesus, it might be good, but it is not church.

This view of the church is intentionally christological. The center of these three components is Jesus. Our commission defines us and calls us to go together, under his authority, to make disciples of all nations. This is what it means to be the church.

We are the church: we represent the life of Christ to the world. Our call, our identity, is a continuation of the ministry of Jesus, who said, "As the Father has sent me, I am sending [all of] you" (John 20:21; "you" is plural). We are sent: we are a part of the apostolic church sent into the world, as he was sent. We continue his work: greater works than these will we do. This does not mean actual miracles that are greater, but together we will do more than he could do as one man, because the way he did ministry (out of relationship) would stay the same for the church, and the church has the ability to be in millions of relationships and in so doing to change the face of humanity.

It might seem harsh to define the church so rigidly. Yet this definition is actually very broad and flexible. Unconsciously we have thought of church more as a building or weekly gathering than as a living, breathing being known by God. Putting a sign that says "church" on the outside of a convenience store or a bank does not make the activities inside that building church. Gathering just to worship, while important and good, isn't enough to be called church. It is worship. Just as gathering believers to worship and even for deep relationships, while important, is not church if those same people don't participate in some way in the Great Commission.

But when any group of people is deeply committed to Jesus, to each other and to the lost, Jesus is there in their midst, and they are church. We will deepen our discussion of what makes simple church and its various expressions in chapter thirteen, but for now it's important to identify what really is church so that we can be sure never to leave it.

Left with Nothing

Much of what leavers leave is not church. We receive criticism from external sources and guilt internally because we are told—and we believe—that we are leaving church in this deeper sense. And often leavers do leave church altogether. Those leavers were not really participating in church but in a part of what it means to be church. But by leaving, they now have nothing.

I don't propose that anyone leave the church. That is to say, just as Paul was called into worship, community and mission, we too are forever called to those three things. As long as they are present, we need not feel guilt about leaving anything less. The problem is that many leavers leave a lesser version of church and replace it with even less. This may not be their intention, but frustration with the ideological inadequacies of their church experience leaves them isolated and less connected than before.

If you're in that place, I want to help. If you have left and you're wondering if you did the right thing, it depends. If you have not left but are considering it and you're wondering if that is even an option, the answer is yes, but it depends on how you do it and what your leaving is leading to. If you're in any of these positions, keep reading.

Life after church begins with a vision for something greater, something more pure, more of what God had in mind.

The *Harvard Business Review* recently ran a first-page advertisement with a simple yet compelling pitch: "Losing even one customer is too many." The ad was for "customer driven companies" and proposed to reveal how fourteen such companies "got it right." How intriguing! Could it be that the business world of free-market capitalism could be more sensitive, more concerned about the loss of clientele, than the church? Is it because we think we have a monopoly on God that we run churches indifferent to leavers?

In one sense, we don't need clients, we don't run on the approval of "customers," and certainly the church should be driven by the heart of God and the converts of God, not by the concerns of any one person. Yet the incarnation and the tender ferocity of the God who is revealed in Jesus Christ also teaches us that God is in relentless pursuit of every wayward heart and that he does not tire of loving them. In fact, there is no price God would not pay for the redemption of leavers.

Yet so little attention is paid to those who are leaving. In churches that are seeing growth through conversions, leavers often have even less credibility, as if numerical growth is equivalent to the approval of God. Certainly, if people are coming to Christ in a church, that is a sign of God's favor and God's work. But we can't make the mistake of believing that such a church is immune to neglecting the matters that accompany maturity.

Further, most churches aren't growing through conversions, and ignoring the leavers is tantamount to participating in the decline of the church. We simply have to care about why committed Christians are leaving churches. We have to care because God cares, because our business is to please the God who taught us to bear with those whose faith is weak and to learn from those who are calling for prophetic change. We need some churches that will say, "Losing even one is too many."

Ironically, good companies care about disaffected customers because they realize it's often these customers that understand the company in a way it can't understand itself. Disgruntled customers have profoundly valuable information for a company looking to innovate, improve or serve clientele in a more complete way. After throwing out the statistical extremes, the church has in its leavers a better vision of itself. At their best (principled and not petty), leavers have insight into how the church can more fully embody the kingdom of God and present the gospel of that kingdom to the unbelieving world. Leavers should know that their vision matters. Because it does.

As a leaver, the temptation can be to imagine that the church and our experience with it is all flaws. We tend to be overly critical in our appraisal of our church experience, defining it strictly in terms of what was wrong, unbiblical or inconsistent. Leavers need to find ways to redirect those experiences into positive vision for something constructive. Instead of talking about what didn't happen in the past, leavers need to use those failed experiences to talk about what can happen in the future.

The first approach only further divides the body of Christ, and leavers are perceived as unfair critics, whining about what they don't like. But if you're a leaver, there is more to your experience. If you're willing to explore, your negative experience can become something redemptive and creative.

Vision is the beginning of leavers' hope. We have to embrace the prophetic insight God can give us as leavers and channel that insight into constructive, kingdom-affirming vision. In other words, we need to talk more about what can be than what was not. If you left a church just because of something it was not, you left for the wrong reasons. If you left a church because, buried beneath your concern about what was missing, you longed for something greater—something God himself longs for—then your leaving could be very meaningful and turn out to be the next step on a journey closer to God, deeper into community and more effectively into his mission. Without a vision or hope, we aren't prophetic; we are just critical.

Historically God has given the same message to many unrelated groups at the same time, validating that message as prophetic. Today many unconnected leavers resonate with a common vision. I've shared ideas about life after church with many people who seem to experience a deep resonance with certain ideas about the church they hope for. This section is an attempt to articulate some of those unifying ideas.

In other words, these ideas and this vision isn't simply a dispassionate depiction of data gathered from leavers. It is my own waking dream—and the dream of many others—of what the church can be. For that reason, I write about these things not as a reporter of facts but as a communicator of a message, albeit flawed, that I hope is from God.

Between the churches we are leaving and the churches we must build lie the churches of our dreams. And that is where we will tread now.

5

THE PEOPLE OF GOD

*T*he people of God are powerful. Whether described as the chosen people, the remnant or the church, these are people God seems to favor in all of his creation. Likewise these are people he builds into a new kind of temple that will glorify him in a way that no human creation can. The complexity, wonder and difficulty of human relationships seem only to magnify the glory of God's work in and through us. Leavers' vision for the church often has a lot to do with respecting and unlocking the power of God in the people of God.

The Priesthood of All Believers

Some of the most beautiful and mysterious passages in the Bible come from the book of Revelation. Although it offers a view of the future, John's apocalyptic book generates more questions than answers. Yet for all his symbolism and strange apocalyptic imagery, John offers us a very real look at heaven and the seat of the government of God. For that reason, Revelation 4–5 inspires endless questions for me. Each realization or revelation that comes from witnessing this heavenly worship confounds me.

Here, for instance, you have God and the Lamb unveiled for all eyes to see. No more obscurity about the true nature of God, his power, his love, his radiance. Creatures, so marvelous that one might be tempted to worship them, surround the throne of God, hailing him as holy, worthy, beautiful. And it isn't compulsion that drives them. They are simply amazed; it's their joy to repeat the praise that with each breath seems infinitely new to them.

There is no mistaking that this is the God who created the universe and who now sits ready to judge what he has created with justice and truth. Yet in the midst of this revelation of true, unrivaled power, we also see twenty-four inscrutable thrones. In the throne room of God's unveiled power sit twenty-four other thrones.

At first, I simply could not understand this. How is it that God would allow rival seats of power in his presence? In the place of God's rule, he has no counselors, no subsidiaries. He is God and it is time for him to take his place. Yet part of the manifold praise lavished on God is that he is King of kings and Lord of lords. And so these "elders" sit as kings in his presence. They aren't stripped of power in his presence, but rather they are given vestiges of their own rule as extensions of his government. They are given crowns to place on their heads and thrones to sit on, and presumably kingdoms still to rule. Could it be that his power is somehow magnified by the presence of other kings?

Granted, they don't really sit on their thrones much. At least that isn't the impression given. Mostly they bow down and worship, because these kings have been made wise by the revelation of the true King: the Lamb that was slain. But I still find it remarkable that God is not threatened by the presence of other leaders and that his leadership is in fact defined by the empowerment of other leaders. He isn't hogging it all for himself.

Perhaps there is a hint in the nature of the Lamb himself. This is a God who is full of love and wrath and who is exemplified by a lamb led to the slaughter. Jesus teaches us, all of us would-be leaders, once and for all that real power isn't found in the exercise of authority but in giving it up. Jesus freely gives his life, and that is exactly what makes him worthy to open the seals of judgment. Deeper than that, this sacrificial gesture reveals not just the strength of Jesus but also the character of God himself. Seen here in the throne room, God is strong enough to share power. He is great enough to empower lesser creatures to lead with him—under him to be sure, but nevertheless really leading. This theophany has completely changed my understanding of leadership.

In the song that these empowered elders sing, they say, "You have made us to be a kingdom of priests to serve our God and king" (Revelation 5:10). If this is the vision of God for his church—a kingdom of priests—should it not be ours? Where then is the expression of this in churches, where leadership is rarely shared and even sometimes hoarded for years by only a few?

Every believer. We leavers envision a church that calls all believers into leadership and service. All have something they can do, people they can influence. This means not simply expecting everyone to fulfill a role related to the programs of the church but encouraging people to discover and develop their God-given identity, becoming who God is calling them to be.

I realize this is a complicated subject. Most church leaders would agree that people should get involved in the activities of the church. They also welcome leadership and service, and they lament the low percentage of their parishioners who actually participate in the life of the church as leaders and servants.

Here is the problem. Most churches set up an infrastructure that is both irrelevant and unattractive to their people, all of whom have unique gifts and abilities. We create structures that need certain kinds of service and leaders and then expect every kind of person to be fulfilled by a handful of opportunities. If you don't want to teach Sunday school or work in the nursery or be an usher or sing in the choir, there's really nothing for you to do. What about the savvy entrepreneur with a heart for the poor? He can become a greeter or, maybe some-day, if he holds on long enough, he could become an elder. But is that really what God has called and equipped him to do? For women in particular (who make up 60 percent of the church), there are truly few options.

Instead of designing churches around programmatic con-victions, leavers dare to wonder if churches should exist to em-power every believer to find and exercise their gifts for the king-dom. We imagine the church as the most flexible enterprise on earth, one that empowers leader-ship and service as diverse as the people involved. In a practical sense, the affirmation of the priesthood of all believers is a re-turn to the apostolic origins of the church. It opens the door for expansion and hope for both a deeper level of fulfillment of be-lievers and more effective mission to nonbelievers.

Every leader. It stands to rea-son that if God in his throne room surrounds himself with a team of leaders, our church gov-ernments ought to do the same. In the wake of the decline of mainline denominations and the emergence of independent churches, there has been an unfor-tunate side effect. Generations of mainline thinking helped to create balanced (for the most part) ecclesial government that prevented the misuse of authority. However, these structures aren't known for their efficiency. In fact, a lot of church humor

> *We are being dehumanized; we don't want to think for ourselves and when we do, it is seen in opposition with the mainstream. The things that get airtime are what one person—the man at the pulpit—believes. One wonders if they even care about what God cares about. Or the more likely assumption: they prepared last minute this morning during worship.*
>
> CRYSTAL

(which isn't really funny to me) is about the organizational inefficiency of committees, boards and other such bureaucracies. Be that as it may, independent church movements have tended to correct these inefficiencies at times with too much reliance on one leader.

My community and I had the privilege to live and work among the urban poor in Metro Manila for nine months. During that time, we worked very closely with a group of church-planting pastors called Missions Ministries Philippines (MMP), working only in the slums. Coming in with some experience working with and among the poor, I was amazed at their longevity, especially considering most of them had been doing this for ten to fifteen years. I was fascinated by how these men and women could work in some of the harshest slum communities in the world and yet have so much joy, such deep friendships and so little ego.

While I was in Manila, I sat on their executive leadership team. Robert, the director, refused to make decisions without his team. The only exception was when it would have been a hardship for them to participate in the decision. Every year they held an election; they looked around the room at each other and asked who should hold the executive role that year. For eight years, they chose Robert, mostly because he seemed to be the best choice, and he was the most willing. Ego seemed as distant a concept as Dr. Pepper and a good Cuban sandwich (items that I regrettably had to do without during my time in Manila). They were all willing to lead and all willing to be led. They were a team. They understood that someone would need to hold the executive position, but they simply did not see it as a position of status or power. They loved each other, worked through their problems like a family and committed themselves to doing whatever they could to plant as many churches in the slums as possible. Team leadership is real.

Leavers like me dream about the end of the single-leader

church. It isn't that there is not a place for executive leadership; someone has to have the final word. But not the only word. Too many churches either stifle their leaders or acquiesce to them. It's possible to imagine and hope for every person in the church to be a part of leading it, in proportion to their calling and investment. We can rethink church government so that people are supported and protected by the design of community.

Leadership outside community is not only unhealthy for the lone leader (and the community she leads), but also limits the work of the Holy Spirit. Single-leader churches expect the gifts of the whole body to be evident in the one leader. This is both unrealistic and unhealthy. The Holy Spirit gives gifts to all for the building of the body, which should never be restricted or encumbered by the monopoly of the one. Because Jesus appointed a team of leaders over the first church, and they in turn also appointed leaders as a team (people who were known to be full of the Holy Spirit), it stands to reason that the contemporary church should also be led by a team of trusted and reputable leaders.

This structure is not only biblical, but it also affords the leader more accountability and less pressure, more creativity and less error, more gifts used for the church and less one-dimensional teaching, more of the Bible with fewer blind spots, more faith, more prayer and more joy. Churches will be happier and more holy if they are led by teams.

We dream of having pastors who are neither subject to another ruling body nor above them, but part of them. Apostolic leaders will lead teams of leaders who listen to everyone who is invested. We hope to find ways to affirm and enjoy the benefits of leadership communities.

Every ethnicity. Another lesson learned from the account of the end of all things (Revelation) is that we will all one day worship as a multiracial, multilingual, multiethnic community. If

we consider the prayer that Jesus taught us to pray—"Your will
be done on earth as it is in heaven" (Matthew 6:10)—it's safe to
assume that this is the will of God not just for heaven and the
future but for the church on earth in the here and now.

It's odd that most churches pray this prayer but don't pursue the simplest, most obvious element of life "as it is in
heaven." Churches in North America have functioned more ef-
ficiently, worshiped more uniformly and interacted more har-
moniously precisely because we have worked to maintain homogeneous churches. This may serve to make churchgoers
more comfortable, but leavers of a new generation are finding
that a vision for a more complicated, more difficult and more
biblical multiethnic church is something we have to work toward. Because music and preaching is so racialized, the church
is finding it difficult (even when it wants to pursue diversity)
to attract people who are different. If you want to attract a certain kind of person to a worship service, you had better create
a worship service that makes sense to them culturally. That includes but is not limited to who is on the stage, the style of music, the style of preaching and even the atmosphere of the
place. If it's too casual, it will seem irreverent to some; if it's
too high church, it will seem pretentious to others. What is a
service planner to do?

There is really only one way to build a church that is truly
multiethnic: we have to make our purpose for being a church
something other than Sunday-morning services. This is consistent with the vision for church that leavers have. We want to
make church about something other than a once-a-week spiritual high, an experience designed to meet our specific consumer needs. If that is what church is about, we will never succeed in maintaining real diversity of any kind. Churches have
to be about more. I can survive and even appreciate a worship
service that is different from what I'm used to or what I like, if
I feel I'm honoring my best friend or making the gospel more

accessible to someone I love. I can occasionally sit through a message that isn't geared to me if I know it's piercing the heart of a nonbeliever I brought or helping to lay a foundation for a loved one to find Jesus. Meaningful mission and the hope for multiethnic community can bring out the best in us as we put aside our own preferences for the sake of others.

We can't have diversity in our churches by simply tweaking our services. We have to pursue crosscultural, crossethnic relationships at more basic levels. Our leaders have to reflect the kind of church we want to build. Our small-group gatherings and our friendships have to reflect a desire for deeper relationships that will build a foundation for a multiethnic church. We should not expect the most relationally superficial expression of church (the weekly worship service) to do it. Crosscultural relationships are a feature of the new church that we must pursue.

We hope for a church that can correct the impression that it's a harbinger of racism (which it has been and at times still is), rigidity, political uniformity and group-think. The bride of Christ was intended to be beautifully diverse, and we aren't displaying that beauty and releasing the full force of the testimony of the cross as long as we are in homogeneous churches.

For twelve years I owned two houses in the inner city that sat side by side and served as the location for this kind of experimental community (one for men and one for women). Year after year we took applicants for a new generation of college students who not only wanted to live closer to the poor but also wanted to live together in a multiethnic community. Leading a dozen of these communities has convinced my heart of one thing: this kind of reconciliation and friendship is not only possible, it also is beautiful.

In all those years, I witnessed more conflicts than you can imagine. Lots of hurt feelings, miscommunication and sin. This kind of community isn't easy. But no one ever left. They never walked away from each other. And these houses have always been a beacon in the neighborhood. The floors are literally bending from all the dancing and parties and joy that have burdened their old structures. This is the paradox of joy and pain, glory and suffering. Whatever the church is called to do will lead to immeasurable glory for God and joy for us. But it will certainly cost us. Of the more than one hundred students who have lived in these houses, many have gone on to live in intentional community. Almost all of them are deeply committed to the vision of the multiethnic church, because they know firsthand that it's possible.

The Insidious Power of One

Our ministry of planting microchurch communities in the inner city has taught me that building ethnically diverse, Christian community is easy to ascend to intellectually but very difficult to actually do. Although racial reconciliation is a very complex issue, in the end it comes down to love. Why don't we love all people? Why is there fear, prejudice and sometimes even hatred in all of us? I've become convinced that the opposite of loving people is not hating people, it's loving ourselves, and that self-serving, self-defining love is the enemy of real racial reconciliation. Often racial prejudice—and the injustice that spills out when power is involved—is derived not from the love of one's own racial group but from the love of oneself alone.

Self-centeredness isn't just an individualized sin. It becomes corporate. If you love only yourself, live for yourself, protect yourself, you will project that love only onto the people who look like you, think like you and act like you. Those whom you perceive as less like you, those who don't reflect your thinking and sensibilities back to you are—at times consciously and at other times subconsciously—perceived as foreign and therefore a threat. People who are different, even physically, challenge our values, culture and choices. For this reason they are too often considered dangerous, to be feared and, when we are at our worst, even destroyed. It's as if the very existence of someone different is a kind of critique of who we are. Racism betrays our narcissism and reveals mental instability as it conceals the myopia of our self-centeredness and paranoia. And I can know that and still fear what is different.

I moved into inner-city Tampa in the spring of 1996. It was a decision I made gladly and have never regretted. What some call a ghetto has really been more like a garden. We've seen some crazy things and even been the victims of crimes, but all of that seems small in the light of the people we have met, the pain we've shared and the love that's been cultivated in us. We never thought that simply choosing to live in a harder place, a place with more struggles, would actually draw us closer to Jesus, as we have seen him at work in our neighborhood. Living there introduced us to another culture, a way of life that is different from and in many ways better than the suburban middle class way of life we were used to.

I'm grateful to God for our neighborhood and the impact it has had on me, and I've never publicly said that other Christians should make the choice I have. I simply believe it has been good for me. Yet very often, when I meet someone new and they hear where we have chosen to live, they can seem a little defensive. I try to put them at ease, letting them know that living in the suburbs is also a valid choice. But because it's clear, theologically thought-out and done with conviction, people often feel challenged by my choice. It just makes some people uncomfortable.

Mostly our choices are a mirror reflecting back to others their own choices, and the implications of those choices. I've never meant to induce hostility, but I get it because my life is a mirror for them just as theirs is for me. I should be in a white, middle-class neighborhood and I'm not; this difference instigates fear and mistrust. That is what difference does to us when we are focused on ourselves.

Egocentrism isn't just an individual problem. It is the enemy of all that is possible as the people of God. When we are too focused on our identity as an individual, we become suspicious and ungracious toward everyone else. There's a reason Jesus said that those who would follow him must deny themselves. It's actually the precursor to saving faith, to following Jesus at all.

A part of the vision that leavers have for the church is seeing the church as more than a collection of individuals. We see it as something that includes all kinds of people because we need their gifts and their ways of looking at the world. Differences between us are exactly what make us beautiful and necessary; together we are more than we were apart. There is a kind of power that comes from respecting the people of God, the priesthood of all believers, and from letting people serve and lead and operate in the role God has assigned for them.

Church can be something bigger precisely because it's the bringing together of so many people with so many reflections of the image of God. It's also big because it is, then, a tool for our redemption out of our selfishness.

Bigger Than Me

I, for one, am tired of thinking only about myself. I'm boring. I used to be so fascinated by my seemingly endless neuroses and the contours of my many quirks. But who cares? I know that no one else really does, so maybe it's a kind of sanity that I'm only now realizing, agreeing with everyone else on planet Earth that my intricacies aren't that interesting. Not to say that God doesn't care about those intricacies. I actually think he does, but when we're talking about me and God in the same sentence, the question of capacity screams to be addressed.

God can care about every hair on our heads because he is infinitely capable. He delights to see the redemptions going on in you and me every day. At the same time God isn't distracted by that, forgetting to care about the lost or my kids or Rwanda, or forgetting to have the sun come up. I, on the other hand, being quite limited in my capacity, tend to be very distracted by my whining heart. If I'm wronged, I can spend hours thinking about it, but in the end all that has really happened is I've forgotten my purpose (or perhaps never realized it in the first place).

Church can be bigger than the individuals who comprise it. Some call that synergy. I call it liberation. How long will we live under the tyranny of our self-serving lifestyles? I'm very interested in something that will lead my heart and the hearts of a community into the burning center of the heart of God—a place where, as Daniel discovered, you're not burned up or burned out but actually see God. That is the point, I guess. We want to see God. Really, we do. But those who long for the new wineskin want others to see him too—maybe even first.

To love the poor and to love the lost and, really, to love any one at all ahead of ourselves is an invitation into the character of God. It's an invitation into wholeness. Freud was wrong. It's not all about your mother or your father just as it's not about what's wrong with you. It's about saying yes to the invitation to follow. It's a simple reality that becomes more and more obscured by spiritual aging. We do not mature in Christ, because we do not follow him. We only age, stepping every day closer to spiritual death. But when we follow, we grow, we mature, we step away from the lure of selfish gain and are wooed to follow the love that gives itself for its enemy. We are drawn into the courts of royal servanthood in all its grit and splendor. We really don't need psychoanalysis; we need psycholiberation, and that comes in the awe of the Master.

When I follow him, he leads me to a place of service, concern and even sacrifice for others. Really, anyone will do. But it's especially powerful when it's the poor who become the object of our focus, because they are the object of God's focus and the fulcrum of his liberating initiative in the world. The margins are calling us because Jesus is already there.

There are two worlds: the world inside our heads, where we are the center, even the creator, the diviner of reality; and the "everything else" world, where we are only a part, a beloved and significant part, but just one part. In this world outside our heads, God is the center, the Creator, the definition of all things. This is the bigger world. This is the start of something big because it's an invitation to follow Jesus into that big world where he is the Lord and King.

Real church has power because people don't usually cooperate on things. Not really, not if there is nothing in it for them. If this vision awakens something in you, and you want to say yes to a version of church that isn't about you per se, then you can. Even wanting that is the start of a new kind of church, because it's the triumph of the cross in you and in those of us who agree. It's the exertion of the power of God to extract us from the current of our culture and to make us into something new. It's the beginning of real church, because it's God who prompts our hearts to act, to join, to cooperate. And it could be leaving that has brought us to this point of finding life after church.

6

THE WORD OF GOD

Shortly after becoming a Christian, I was given one of those gold Good News Bibles. I had seen some other Christians I knew write in theirs, underlining and making notes in the margins, so I thought that was how you demonstrate you really study the Bible. Every night I would read that Bible, underlining words or phrases that stuck out to me and making notes about each part's significance. Several years of Bible reading each night left that Bible tattered and marked on every page. I can remember a certain kind of immature pride in it. When people would pull out their Bible at a church service or Bible study, I always did so with a little flare.

In my senior year of college, I was leading a Bible study on the book of James. Each week I would prepare for that study in the same way. Pulling out my old Bible, I would start by reading my own notes accumulated in its margins.

Then I got to James 5. I was stunned. There was no mark or comment of any kind in the whole chapter. It just sat there, naked, unnoticed, brutally ignored. Certainly I would have read through the book of James a dozen times over the years. I never found anything noteworthy? I couldn't believe it.

Once I'd read that chapter I was again shocked by the content I had never thought significant enough to underline or comment on. It was a rude awakening to the reality of a personal blind spot. I hadn't considered that the content of James

5 applied to me. But reading through it this time, I understood, perhaps in a way I never had, that it's the unmarked places of the Bible that hold some of the most relevant and challenging words.

It could be said that each reader of the Bible reads with personal blinders. There are blind spots that we simply can't overcome by trying harder. Churches that form themselves in the context of culture have cultural blind spots too, leaving entire groups of Christians missing important pieces from the mosaic of God's self-revelation.

When we apply Scripture—really believe it and integrate it into our lives—it becomes written on our hearts. This is, I believe, the ultimate value of Scripture for us: that it would not just be something we read to know but something we read to live. When that process becomes about doing and living our theology, we have appropriated Scripture as the living Word. This living Word written in the honesty of our hearts is often an edited word, omitting certain parts of the revealed Word in Scripture.

That was true for me and James 5. It was in the Bible I read but not the Bible I lived. James 5 had been omitted from the Bible in my heart and for that reason held a key to a new understanding of the love of God for the poor and the revelation of God as just.

My personal omission betrays not only a personal blind spot but a cultural one as well. In all my years going to myriad white, evangelical churches, I've still to this day never heard a sermon or even a reference to the book of Amos. In the first church service I attended overseas (in Haiti), the message was on Amos. The first black church I attended in this country also had a sermon on Amos. How can we explain that? What's in Amos that seems so relevant to some but so irrelevant to others? Maybe even now you're not sure of the answer to that question because you don't know what the book of Amos says.

And so the cultural conspiracy continues.

Leavers dream of a church that's ruthless against its own ignorance. We imagine a church where we read the Bible for all it has to say and give special attention to the places that make us the most uncomfortable or that challenge our current way of thinking. We hope for a kind of church that practices an organizational humility, looking for ways to learn from other cultures and other kinds of churches because we know that God is revealing himself to them as well, and perhaps they have an openness to see him in ways we find difficult.

Too often the Bible is simply a tool we use to confirm ideas we already hold. There's scarcely a more theologically destructive habit. It's hard to believe that people so committed to God would be so unsure about his Word. Without Scripture the church is adrift with no sense of direction. In that condition we are just as likely to sail into the dangerous waters of convenient personal theology as we are to find our way to the truth. It's simply impossible to imagine a church remaining true to the way of Jesus without a commitment to the Bible as it is.

> *The focus was always on what we needed to stop doing and never what we ought to be doing. There wasn't much mention of Christ's redemptive power or how to tap into that. This combination caused me to feel hopeless because it put the onus of perfection on me and I knew that wasn't working. The only reason I ever went back was guilt.*
> DAN

The trouble, of course, is that most Christians affirm the Bible as central, yet they don't make it central to their practice in preaching, teaching or life application. Many leavers find this discrepancy frustrating. Ironically, because mere lip service

often is paid to the value of Scripture, congregants are empowered to question and measure the teaching and practice of a
church's leaders and programs. Often it's the Bible that produces the fires of discontentment in leavers. They have trouble
living with the dissonance they experience between what they
read in the Bible and what they see in their churches.

What I would read in the unmarked pages of my Bible—
places like James 5, Amos and the other minor prophets—
would change my life forever. Reading them with an open
heart revealed new insights into the words of Jesus and what
he really meant, into what the gospel and the kingdom are
about. I can't do justice to the impact these Scriptures have
had on the direction of my life in ministry and the way they
have taught me about God.

We will need spiritual bravery to face God for who he says
he is. Light has come into the world in Jesus Christ. His life,
faithfully rendered in Scripture, has to be preserved not only
in the pages of an ancient document but in the living practice
of the church that bears his name. We honor Jesus as Lord as
we have the courage to explore the places of his life that we do
not live. We need Scripture to teach us, to challenge us and to
humble us. The Bible is more than a guidebook; it's the revelation of God. The church that leavers dream of reads the Bible
hungrily for who we need to be as well as who we can be. The
manipulation of Scripture has to be replaced with a sincere humility as each page and each revelation is treasured as a reflection of our love and obedience to Jesus himself.

It's hard to put into words just how important the Bible has
been and needs to be to the people of God. If we are to know
God, we have to know him as he has presented himself and let
the mirror of his revelation reflect truth into our lives. The tendency to read the Bible as a devotional resource is good but incomplete. The Bible isn't "chicken soup for the soul." Often
it's a scathing critique of the condition of our soul. It's the

best representation of the history of the revelation of God. It isn't simply a book of stories or prophecies or oracles from God or even teachings about how to live. It's all of those things and more. Because the Bible is the best account of the revelation of God, it is to be trusted above every subjective revelation or experience. It is to be the measure of all that we think, feel and do. It is to be the standard for the church and the people who make up churches. For this reason, there has to be a tenacious commitment to the Bible, especially to the testament of Jesus and its centrality in the life of believers and the churches they form.

God Revealing Himself

After I spoke at a university in my city recently, I stayed to answer questions. One junior asked how it was that Jesus could be God when he spoke to God and talked about the Father clearly as someone other than himself. "Can you show me in the Bible," he asked, "where it says that Jesus was God?" I asked him if he had ever learned to do something by watching someone else do that thing. How did that person teach? Wasn't it by demonstrating how to do it? Did they not limit their ability in order to show how to do the most basic technique, to act it out so that you could then try it? He thought of an example and agreed.

One dilemma of the human condition is that we all know that God exists and that we were made for relationship with him, but we are in many ways powerless to engage that relationship. God's transcendence makes him both inscrutable and unapproachable. The Bible says that God lives in "unapproachable light" (see 1 Timothy 6:16). So the only way we will ever satisfy our longing to know God is if God himself is interested in being known and engages us. God can be accurately revealed only by himself. No one can go on a search for God and find him (unless he wants to be found). Think about it: if

God wanted to hide his character, his will, his mind from us, what hope would we have of discovering it?

So, I explained to my new friend that God knows that we would know him, learn how to be human and how to live as human beings in a friendship with God only if he himself took the form of a human being living in friendship with God. If God did not take human form, but took some kind of divine form, we may have learned about him, but we would never have learned how to be ourselves with him. We would never have learned how to be human in relationship to God. This is the miracle and effect of the incarnation. God limited himself in Jesus, not just figuratively but actually, and in so doing he was honestly interacting with himself as a surrendered servant. Jesus talked to the Father as a servant, as one submitted and under authority, although as Philippians 2 points out, he was not a servant by nature; by nature he was God.

I showed my new friend John 1. In the beginning, Genesis says, there was only God. John says in the beginning there was the Word. The Word was both with God and the Word (simply put) was God. John goes on, saying that nothing was made without him; the Word is the Creator. Eventually, John explains, the Word became flesh, and we have seen his glory. The Word, who is God, who is the Creator of all things, became flesh. In the limitation of human flesh, Jesus legitimately lived as a human being, teaching us how to live a submitted life. He teaches us how to be human and how to live in relationship with God.

God, who is not human, teaches us how to be human by becoming human. Very simple. Not really, but it is the case. And we can't be fooled by the reality of Jesus' humanity to believe that he is not also God. He was both. This is certainly not difficult metaphysically to understand because it isn't beyond the scope or power of God to become human. Yet it's one of the most mysterious doctrines, what theologians call the hypostatic union.

We are doomed to grope in the dark for spiritual answers about God and about ourselves unless God illuminates us. And this is the testimony of John: "In him was life, and that life was the light of men" (John 1:14). Jesus is the Word. The Word of God is more than the Bible, but it is not less. And the Bible is the part of the Word that we have preserved. It's the faithfully rendered story of God revealing himself in human history, culminating in the incarnation and the self-revelation of God in Jesus Christ. For this reason the Bible will remain sacred, as the best source for knowing the truth about God and for examining every other kind of revelation.

Our interaction with Scripture is an interaction with Jesus. If we ignore parts of it, we ignore him. If we give Scripture a peripheral place, eventually we will have marginalized Jesus himself. Leavers want an authority that is beyond themselves, beyond the talking heads in the front. We dream of a church grounded in the ancient authority of the Bible and the living Word of God, which is Jesus. Young leavers are mystical enough to know that Jesus is very much alive and still speaking to his church. But if we hold onto that belief without the grounding of Scripture, we are destined to become apostate. We must grip Jesus by every handle he has given us and hold on. The Bible is our lifeline to the future we know is possible.

7

THE MISSION OF GOD

I think the church is a little lost. Still beloved by God, still the light of the world, still so ripe with potential that it can be measured only by the God who remains ready to supply. But I also believe that we have to ask for that supply. The church sits as the only institution with the resources to transform the face of planet Earth to a place of justice, peace and equity, a place without suffering. We have the message (gospel), we have the leader (Jesus), we have the example (sacrifice), and we have the power (love). The church has nevertheless lost its way. On the one hand we are capable of so much, and on the other hand we are accomplishing so little.

The Commissioned Church

We are like a great warrior who has gotten lost on the way to the battle and been gone so long that he has forgotten what he set out to do. All that remain for the warrior are remnants of the original journey. Hanging over the fireplace is his old sword that stayed close for many years but now just hangs, gathering dust, a forgotten weapon of a forgotten mission. A shield is safely stored there, because the lost warrior no longer needs protection from anything; his life is all comfort. This may be why he never got back on his way; he found such comfort in his lostness.

This is the story of the church. Sent by Jesus himself to subdue evil, to destroy all the works of the evil one, to proclaim freedom for the captive and good news for the poor, to declare and establish the triumph of God, we never got there.

We stopped in the city of mediocrity and moderation, and there in the decadence of that city we have forgotten that the city of God is yet to be built. While the rest of the world is wasting away under the tyranny of sin, and hell is having its way with our children, and the poor are sacrificed to the god of material wealth, the church is growing weak and its great weapons—the Word of God and faith—have become sermon titles and concepts relegated to the realm of self-help and personal inspiration.

We have lost our way, and worse, we have forgotten to care. The battle yet rages. Where is the church?

The church exists to do what God created it to do. For that reason the church can never simply *be;* it also has to *do.* We might argue that being comes before doing, but however you get to it, Jesus explained that a tree is known by its fruit. In other words, what we do defines who we are and, of course, who we are defines what we do. I might say and believe that I'm an honest person. So that is my state of being. But if in one particular context (work, for instance) I often stretch the truth with exaggeration or even lie to make myself look good, am I honest? Clearly not—at least not by any measurement that matters. If, when confronted with my chronic dishonesty I respond by saying, "That is not really who I am. I am really a very honest person," what does that mean to the listener? What does it even mean to me? Is it not just another kind of self-deception? They know that at work I'm not particularly honest. There is now what I say I am and what I define myself to be by my actions. My being is, at least in part, defined by what I do.

Likewise the church is defined by what it does in relation to what it has been asked to do and its obedience to or compliance with that directive. We have to return to a definition of church that honors this reality. We have to think about church again as a gathering of people who share the same purpose.

Paul defines the church as Christ's ambassadors, "as though God were making his appeal through us" (2 Corinthians 5:20). This is especially meaningful when we think about the transition that all followers of Jesus are called to make, from disciples to apostle, from student to missionary. I don't mean *missionary* in the formal sense (although certainly many will live this out by making mission their occupation), but as a deeply personal and real self-description. Ambassadors are sent. They do other things besides deliver the message, but they are by definition sent with a message, as a representative for that dignitary.

The question the modern church has to ask itself, and what we as individual believers have to ask ourselves, is this: Are we ambassadors if we are not going? Just as being sent is a necessary condition of being an ambassador (you have to be chosen and then given a message), so going is a necessary condition—unless we are going to create a new kind of category: the ambassador that is sent but does not go. For too many churches, this is the case. We are meant to be defined by the doing of our mission. We are the church because we accept the Great Commission.

> Then the eleven disciples went to Galilee, to the mountain where Jesus had told them to go. When they saw him, they worshiped him; but some doubted. Then Jesus came to them and said, "All authority in heaven and on earth has been given to me. Therefore go and make disciples of all nations, baptizing them in the name of the Father and of the Son and of the Holy Spirit, and teaching them to obey everything I have commanded you. And surely I am with you always, to the very end of the age." (Mathew 28:16-20)

I was recently reflecting on this passage with a group of new college graduates. We were looking at how to make decisions about our future. As we studied this often-quoted yet rarely applied story in Matthew 28, a few things stood out to us.

"They worshiped him; but some doubted." The first oddity about this scene is that worship and doubt commingle in it. It's as if the doubt of some is noteworthy, but it does not disqualify them. Matthew does not even identify the doubters. So why does he mention them at all? Two things are apparent: (1) doubt does not negate worship, and (2) worship is the condition of commissioning, not lack of doubt.

Jesus commissions a bunch of men who both stand in awe of him and his recent resurrection and wonder if he is real. These are the men he commissions for the building of his church, the preaching of his gospel and the salvation of the nations. This is a wonderful element of the Great Commission because it emphasizes surrender to the Master (which we can control) and not perfect mental fortitude (which we can't control). What does it all mean? Jesus commissions ordinary people. His mission is passed on to those who would follow him as master and obey him, not necessarily those who are professionally prepared. He seems more concerned with their availability and submission than with their competency or giftedness, a revelation that is both wonderful and terrifying for ordinary people like you and me.

A Defining Command

Jesus makes his case for why they should go into all the world and make disciples on these grounds: "All authority in heaven and on earth has been given to me." I used to think that Jesus mentioned his authority here because he wanted his friends to know that they have authority. Take, for example, in Matthew 10 when he sends them out and gives them his authority to do what they had seen him doing. But this seems different. Here he notes his authority so that they know he has the right and the position to make the subsequent command. In other words, "I came as God, but was despised and rejected, and I did not fight back. In the end I submitted to death itself and now I have defeated even that. All authority has now been given to me, and I can say what I want to who I want, and they have to do it." The postresurrection Jesus is supreme; he isn't to be denied, and his commands are to be taught and obeyed, especially that we need to teach obedience to every nation.

Why give eleven people such an impossible task? What was Jesus thinking? What would be the function of giving such an enormous task to a person or a group of people, a task for which they were so obviously inadequate? Was it not simply to convince them once and for all that this relationship with Jesus did not end with his going? That his ascension was really just the beginning for them and that it would take the rest of their lives and all their energy to even begin to fulfill what he was asking of them?

Jesus was defining the rest of their lives with this command. He was defining their method (disciple making) and their reward (his presence). What we discovered in our recent reading was just how freeing this command is. So much of our lives (if they are committed to Jesus) are spent trying to discern whether this or that thing is what I'm supposed to do. But here Jesus is giving a command by which every decision can be measured. All decisions, in a way, can be boiled down to this question: Is this going to help us fulfill our commission? Jesus has supplied us with a clear mission for which all other endeavors should be subservient.

I asked the graduates to think about it like this: What if Jesus were to speak to you personally and undeniably, and to tell you, "My will for you is to find a cure for cancer"? Assuming that you're sure it was God communicating with you and assuming that you're fully committed to obeying God, wouldn't this command settle a lot for you? On the one hand, you have a seemingly impossible task before you. I know if he said that to me I would have a lot of work to do to even begin to know how to do that (for example, go to medical school, get a research grant and so on). This one clear command would re-define you. On the other hand, you would always know who you are, what it is you were created to do. On those days when things were dark or difficult, you would at least know that you were doing what you were called to do. That clarity, we all agreed, while a heavy burden, would be a great gift to us.

In my view, this is exactly what Jesus is doing with the Great Commission—not just for the eleven disciples, but for every-one who would ever call themselves a follower of Jesus. With this enormous goal, he is defining us and our life's pursuit. In that sense he is saying that who we are will be defined by what we do.

The mission is for us in that it connects us to the one who sends us. The promise that Jesus ends with is perhaps the great-est reward a worshiping follower could ask for: the presence of the Master. There is simply no greater offer that Jesus could make. He commits: "Do my mission and I will be with you."

Of course, the irony of this promise can't be ignored. Jesus was saying this just before he would leave the disciples forever. Physically he would never be with them again. Not as they were, sitting on that mountain, where they had so many memories of listening to him teach and watching him reveal God. This was the end of that kind of presence. But Jesus was still promising that he would be with them, but that promise now is connected to the adoption of his mission and the defining of themselves as his, even when he wouldn't be physically present.

I don't know any other way to put this: The church has been sent, and we are a people whose community is defined by the task we have been given. But too many expressions of church have wandered from this task. Too often we have settled for life without mission or redefined the mission to meet our own needs.

Christian Narcissism and the Death of Mission

Radical leavers dream of a church that isn't just about them. Many of us are tired of being coaxed into the maze of meeting our own needs; we never find our way to the end. The whole world seems to be saying, "Look out for yourself; take care of yourself; satisfy your every desire." And the church is no different. The pressure we feel is to find a church that meets our needs, feeds us, gives us what we want. It isn't just that we are consumers but that we are self-indulgent. The ethic of our consumption is satisfaction, which is contrary to the very essence of the gospel and the way of Jesus.

I'm part of a young but powerful missional community. We are the church, though that isn't always recognizable in the traditional sense. We don't have a building, and so much of who we are is a work in progress. I will say more about this community, but when we were first forming, I could not help but sense that we were doing something significant, something profoundly biblical. We were planting a church with nothing decided. Humility, listening and openness were our primary values. The fifty people who agreed to set out on such an undefined quest all shared one very powerful characteristic: surrender of their own agenda. In the beginning, that is what defined us: surrender to God and his mission. The best thing about being missional is the liberation from the tyranny of constant self-interest.

The ancient story of Narcissus has haunting modern application for the church. This Greek myth tells the tale of a man whose beauty is matched only by his vanity and pride. Scorning the love of a woman, Narcissus happens one day upon his own reflection in the water. Smitten with his own image, he falls in love with the reflection he sees and is unable to ever leave. His vanity and love of his own image becomes his demise as he wastes away on the riverbank.

We have become so enamored with our own urges, self-understanding and felt needs that we can scarcely think of anything else. Churches that want to grow and succeed seem to need to cater or capitulate to this vanity. But leavers, in part, have left because they want church to be about something more significant. I don't want a church to cater to me as the consumer. I want the church to fulfill its mission and help me find a way to be a part of it. The irony is that, of all our needs, the one most profound is our need to fulfill our God-given identity and calling. Being engaged in the mission of God, fulfilling the commission God has given to you and me, is our destiny. It's the thing that will most satisfy us. Despite what we may feel from time to time, it's much better to focus our attention outward than to fall in love with the reflection of our own desires. Fixating on our own needs will lead only to our demise.

We were made for mission. We were made to experience community built on something more solid than common needs. We were made to experience church as the call to something other than ourselves, as an invitation into the Great Commission. This is a hope that leavers are chasing in their life after church.

> *We're told not to go where the non-Christians are because (1) it's potentially dangerous and (2) we should be in church. We should be in church as much as we can: Wednesday night service, Sunday morning service, Saturday morning (7am!) men's group, a small group, etc. Where are the relationships with those not in the church? It's almost as if we put the evangelism on God. No seeking at all, just waiting.*
>
> DAVE

8

THE KINGDOM OF GOD

*T*ry to imagine a world where parents love each other, where there is no betrayal, no infidelity, only growing respect, appreciation and love for each other. Then imagine the children born to these parents and growing up surrounded by the same kind of people, where they are nurtured, inspired, allowed to be creative and challenged to be disciplined. Imagine kids honoring and admiring their parents and growing up to become like them.

Imagine friendships no longer weighed down by broken promises or unfair expectations, where race is a perfume that follows each friend, making us love our differences and not fear them. Where people walk around generally whole, ready to serve or give. Where needy people never go uncared for, because everyone wants to be the one to help. Where trust is a basic assumption underlying all new relationships. Where some people get married because they really like to be together and some don't because they are completely fulfilled by the seemingly limitless pool of people who love them, by deep friendships and by meaningful work.

Imagine a world where bosses make you feel that your work matters and at the same time inspire you to work harder and be better. Where people give their whole hearts to their work because they love what they do, believe in it at a deep level and are good at it. Where workers give their best to everything they do. And why wouldn't they?

This is a world where you rarely wait in lines. Where people take their time because the point is to do it right, not to beat out the other guy. It's a world where fast-food restaurants all go out of business because food is cooked with care and shared, and everyone eats meals with company. Where no one is lazy, no one needs therapy, everyone is so happy with who they are and how they look that no one overeats or diets—just lots of people in various cool sizes.

Imagine a world where there is health, inside and out. Where people get it. Where everything isn't perfect; there are still misunderstandings and occasional problems, but these are all handled with grace and fairness and, above all, love.

This is the kingdom of God, and it is coming and has come.

I know that one day this will be the world as we know it, because Jesus has come and finally established his kingdom everywhere. But what about now? What about in my heart? Can the kingdom be normative there? What about my family? Can the kingdom come there, now? If the answer to those questions is yes, I also want to hope that it can come in congregations, communities and even cities.

If the dream that leavers have for church could be confined to one term, it would be *the kingdom of God*. It's the gospel of the kingdom that Jesus preached, not simply a propositional truth about his life and death on the cross but a picture of the new order that would be ushered in by his sacrifice and power. Jesus and his work are the epicenter of the earthquake that is the kingdom. For this reason the kingdom is gospel (good news) for all who are dispossessed, wanting, needy, abused and forgotten. It's good news because its message contains not only a promise for the salvation of those who would believe, but a reorganization of the world as we know it into the likeness of the government and charity of heaven. The kingdom is a promise about the righting of all things wrong and the final defeat of evil, fear and pain. It's the product of the goodness of God being unleashed to rule the world. Therefore leavers should and often do care about the poor of the earth. The longing for more is the shared longing of all who know there should be more. It's the longing for the kingdom to come.

The Immense Kingdom

The kingdom of God offers us a vision that encompasses the whole world. It is unrivaled in sheer scope. Jesus was preaching a gospel as big as his Father and as big as the hunger of the human heart. Every Christian has a hunger inside her, a longing that comes from every encounter she has ever had with God. This longing is often unregistered by the conscious mind, but it's there nevertheless. Once we know God and are known by him, we are rewired to hunger for more.

I'm an activist by nature. It's hard for me to sit and write, but I've been moved to write this book because I want leavers who are leaving churches due to an unrequited love, a longing that is too great for words, to know they aren't crazy. I want them to know that some of what they're feeling is hunger that is from God. It's a hunger for his kingdom; it's the heart praying the Lord's Prayer: your kingdom come, your will be done on earth as it is in heaven. This is the destiny of humanity; it's the destiny of the world. It fills our dreams, but it also emerges in our lives. The kingdom in its fullness may not be possible now, but in small doses it's already here. It is the expansion of the grace and justice of the kingdom we long for.

Saving the Streets, Not Just the Kids on Them

Mostly we have thought of church as an alternative. Think about targeted ministry, such as ministry to kids in the inner city or youth ministry in general. Too often the stated goal is "to get these kids off the street." We see the dangers in youth culture and the temptations of deviant behavior, and we conclude that ministry to them should provide another place to go, an alternative. But the kingdom proposes to save the streets along with the kids who play on them. We don't bring our ministry to the streets anymore because we don't believe they can change. The streets are lost. And we are afraid. So we save as many kids as we can by getting them into the church. We even call our places of worship "sanctuaries."

By and large, our ecclesial structures have become bomb shelters, places to hide from the world we believe is doomed for destruction, places stocked with Christian canned goods for the coming disaster. We think that being church means providing an alternative to the world. It's as if we believe that God has jammed a stick of dynamite into the earth and is just waiting to light it. Since the world will soon be incinerated, we turn our heads, plug our ears and hold on until that day comes.

I imagine a scene on a street corner, where onlookers stand to watch as a building burns. Someone tries to walk into the burning building, and the Christians say, "That building is burning. You may not be able to see the flames from this angle, but trust me, the fire has started and it's burning down. Don't go in there. Come into our building instead."

The person replies, "But what about the building? All my stuff is in there, all my friends, my family, my cat."

To which we respond, "We told them not to go in too, but they didn't listen to us."

"Shouldn't someone do something?"

"They can come here whenever they want. Our building is open to everyone."

"Is that a fire hose connected to your building?"

"Oh yes, we have one of those. You can never be too careful with fires breaking out everywhere. We have that in case some of the fire touches our building."

"Why not use your fire hose to help put out the fire?"

"But if we did that, no one would want to come to our building anymore. We would all be safe."

Exactly.

We aren't an alternative for the world. Our ministries can't
seek simply to inoculate the world from the disease of sin or
to shelter them from the storm of evil. We do that, but we
also look to cure the disease and calm the storm. These are
perfect jobs for our Messiah, for whom healing the sick and
manipulating nature was common. We are agents of transformation who have been sent into the world to lovingly change
it. We are sent to put out the fire, to save the whole building
so that every place is a place where God dwells. This is the
gospel of the kingdom of God, and this is the kind of ministry we are called to.

Agents of Impossible Change

Jesus once used the image of a mustard seed to describe the
kingdom of God. He said it is the smallest seed, but when it's
planted, it grows to become one of the largest plants. Why
would he choose this image? Just to illustrate that God can use
something small? Or that what the kingdom produces is something very big? Or both? What we see in the image of the mustard seed is radical, miraculous, revolutionary change. It is a
parable about impossible change. The seed, insignificant and
unnoticed, miraculously becomes something massive and impossible to ignore. Churches are supposed to be mustard
seeds, influencing their world in ways that are disproportion-
ate to their station.

We stand on the threshold between the first and second
coming. In the first, Jesus defined holiness: he lived the perfect life so that we could know how to know God. More than
that, his death made knowing God possible. And now everything is possible. I don't say that because I'm optimistic by nature. I am not. I say that because it's the reality of a world bask-

ing in the light of the incarnation, reeling from the miracle of
the first advent. Equally we stand waiting for his return, when
he finishes what he started, when the revelation of the Son becomes known to all, and the trees and the earth itself wait with
bated breath.

In some mysterious way that's beyond me, we help to usher
that kingdom in. The world as we know it will be destroyed,
but the kingdom of God will remain. We're a part of a cosmic
displacement, a transition from the kingdom of this world,
which will be destroyed with the coming of the kingdom of
love. It is displaced by the proclamation and demonstration of
the kingdom now.

> And this gospel of the kingdom will be preached in the
> whole world as a testimony to all nations, and then the
> end will come. (Matthew 24:14)

> Since everything will be destroyed in this way, what kind
> of people ought you to be? You ought to live holy and
> godly lives as you look forward to the day of God and
> speed its coming. (2 Peter 3:11-12)

The preaching of the good news of this coming kingdom
and the living out of that kingdom now speeds its coming. We
live in the paradoxes that only Jesus can change this world with
his coming and that we can change it now and that the kingdom is both coming and here now. We believe in transformation because it's the destiny of the world, and our faith in that
destiny represents the coming of the kingdom now.

We can go back to the abandoned places because they are
where transformation is needed. We can return to the places
we have abandoned as lost: the ghettos, the marketplace, the
Third World. For a generation, churches have migrated into
the suburbs, a move that has left abandoned the most desperate places in our cities, the places in greatest need of transfor-

mation. For this reason, leavers dream of engineering the church's passage back into the abandoned places, back into the ghettos, back into the realm of the needy. This is where the church belongs, because it's where Jesus is.

The church's move away from these places is both symbolic and formative. On the one hand, it's a symbol of our intellectual and theological movement from the poor and the needs of others toward the "felt needs" of congregants. On the other hand, it's formative in that we are now converting people into a new kind of Christianity that does not include the widow, the orphan or the alien, something that would greatly distress Jesus, James and the first church, to name just a few.

But we feel powerless to change things. We feel we can barely keep our own needs met, our families sane, our kids safe and our lives in submission to God. How can we stand a chance in the hardest places? How could we make a difference against such massive enemies as poverty and injustice?

The problems facing humanity are so great, so complex, that we need solutions on multiple fronts. Solutions would be impossible, except for the mustard-seed principle. Widespread change will be possible only through a revolution of people and their choices. There has to be a conversation of millions of people on a new kind of ethic of forgive-

> *You always know everything in order—no room for anything out of sorts to happen, like a testimony or extended prayer for specific issues in church. They didn't deal with real issues inside, much less outside—missions, poverty, discipleship. Too many rules: women had to wear skirts, no chewing gum, cover your head when you sing on stage, no cutting your hair, nothing sleeveless, no women in leadership.*
>
> STEPHANIA

ness and mercy, and fairness for all people—an ethic of radical love. Who can broker such a revolution? Who has the infrastructure and the sustainable doctrine as well as a leader who is timeless and suitable and adaptable as a hero for all people in all times and all cultures?

The solution is Jesus Christ. Not just Jesus in the life to come, but Jesus today. I'm not speaking a cliché. I'm engaged in pursuing social change and individual change. But it's only the resurrected Jesus who sits ready to rule his body and govern his people and to lead to a revolution of redemption. It is Jesus who has already equipped us with every good thing we need for life and godliness. He has given us the Holy Spirit to speak for us and through us in every situation. He is also powerful enough to bend the machinations of men on a global scale so that if our cause is hindered in some way, he can make a way for his people. He is both accessible to us and also transcendent; he is our Father in heaven. He is our model, our mentor and our hero, while he is also our friend and our brother in the struggle. He is the perfect leader of the perfect cause at the perfect time.

But too often we chose to abdicate our responsibility and give up our place in the revolution because we are content to leave things the way they are. Lesser gods have too often placated us. We aren't effective because we prostitute ourselves and our allegiances for other things.

C. S. Lewis wrote that the devil's greatest trick was to offer us Christianity and . . . It does not matter what we add to it, just that we add something. The mistake we have made is that we have allowed our relationship with Jesus to be one among many, one kingdom among other competing personal and political kingdoms.

I'm not suggesting that you add to your Christianity an agenda. I'm saying as Lewis said that we ought to be content with mere Christianity. Christ and his kingdom alone. Other powers are in play, but our allegiance has to be clear. Government can serve God, and it's right for the government to take care of the poor, to ensure the overall welfare of all the people under its charge. But that isn't enough. It's right for the government to police criminality. But that isn't enough. Only Jesus Christ and his people can deal with the actual problem. We have the power and the knowledge and the mandate to heal the wounds of this world. To say or to act as though we don't is simply wrong. It denies our calling and our true identity.

Jesus said you are the light of the world, you are the salt of the earth. If there is darkness, if there is immorality, if there is pain and injustice, the responsibility is with us, since we are the ones with the solution. We embody the solution. So when you see human frailty, it ought to inspire you to let Jesus' life flow through you more and to organize as many of your friends as possible to create new kinds of structures that are small but just. Businesses, ministries, neighborhood associations, sports teams, even churches can see the kingdom of God come. Just as any collection of sinners will produce unjust systems, so any collection of God's people should or, at the very least could, produce just systems.

Why can't churches start schools that provide a just education, affirming minority contributions to society and telling the truth about history and the dignity of all people?

Why can't the church establish shelters that can serve more than the entire homeless population of a city? And do it in a way that reflects the holiness of the alien instead of marginalizing them further?

Why can't the church of one city provide relief for another in the Third World, taking on the struggle of its people as its own?

Why can't the church set up mentoring and adoption programs that make sure that every child, regardless of race or economic position, has both a father and a mother? And take children without any parents and find homes for them within the church?

Why can't the church set up programs that place the elderly without means into the care of younger families who have both the space and the need to respect and honor the generation that has gone before them?

All this is possible, but leavers don't see it in churches. So we wander and wonder when.

The church that leavers long for offers hope to the world because we have been given the vision of the kingdom, the calling to see that kingdom come and to see the will of the Father accomplished. Whether it happens in our lifetime or if it's even possible isn't our concern. Our concern is to so love this vision that we live for it, that we long for it, that we would die for it.

We believe in a kingdom that isn't colorblind but sees the beauty of each culture and people group, longs for their participation in the corporate worship of God and sees the sin against people of certain skin colors.

We believe in a kingdom where the subjects don't rest until everyone is treated like a human being: loved, respected, forgiven, accepted. Where every child is seen as a bearer of the fingerprint of God. Where the Third World's problems are first priority. Where we fight and scratch and bleed and pray until there is no more child prostitution, no more slave labor, no more racial profiling, no more hate crime.

We believe in a kingdom where little girls look at themselves in the mirror and say, "I am just right." Where little boys fight for the weakest among them and never for themselves. Where hope is alive because we hold before our eyes the vision of Jesus both crucified and risen. Where suffering is our joy because we are found worthy to suffer for Christ. Where, as Jesus did at Gethsemane, we see the price we must pay and pay it, embracing the suffering before us and demonstrating the inexhaustible power of the one who calls us, the one who went before us, the one who receives us—Jesus the Christ.

I, for one, am ready to give all I have to pay any price to drink any cup for the love of his bride, for the sake of his gospel. I am not alone.

EMPOWERED STAYING

Until now, no significant distinction has been made between the readers who may have already left their church and the readers who have done so only on an emotional level. Those still contemplating actually leaving may feel emboldened by what they have read so far. And I think that is good. Others may still be asking, "How do I make such a decision?" Even after all that has been said, still the question lingers: Can leaving the local church ever really be the right thing to do? So I need to say again, yes, it *could* very well be. But that does not mean it *is* the right thing for you to do. As William Hendricks points out in his book *Exit Interviews*, most leavers don't want to leave their churches. I want to affirm that generally this is a very good instinct. For many leavers, leaving is the last thing they want to do, and they go to great pains to stay.

Some of us simply are in church situations that will serve only to deepen our despondency, because change is so unlikely. We need to be in communities that affirm our convictions. Yet we know that no community is perfect and that we need to give grace to groups and leaders if we are ever going to be able to work together for God's purposes.

So, what if you sense that you should stay? This too could be exactly what God is leading you to. For that reason I want to devote this section to how to do that well. If you're debating whether to stay or go, read it. If you're staying, you need to do it in a certain way. But it can be done, and healthy staying could mean new life for you and for your local church.

Further, everyone is called to stay eventually. The point of the leaving journey is to find a way to stay. I want to give people permission to leave if they need to, if God is calling them to, but the point of leaving is to find somewhere to stay. For many of us, we can do that right where we are. Staying is a virtue.

Earlier this year I was given a traffic citation for running a red light. It was one of those situations we've all been in: the light turned yellow at just that point where it would have been difficult for me to stop, but by not stopping I ended up in the middle of the intersection as the light turned red. The rules of the road are that when you see a yellow light, you're required to stop "if you can do so safely." I had to make a split-second judgment, and I went for it. I contested the ticket.

So many people are sitting in weekly church gatherings seeing spiritual yellow lights. What I'm suggesting is that you stay if you can do so safely. Stay if you can stay in a spirit of cooperation, growth and hope for the future. But if you can't stay safely, if you can't stay in that way, you ought to keep driving. It's really better for both you and the other drivers on the road if you keep going through some yellow lights. I think I could not have stopped safely, so I knew I had to keep driving through that intersection. It seems dangerous, but hitting the brakes at that point could have been more dangerous.

9

HOW TO STAY
AND FIND JOY

*I*t's vital that if someone is going to stay, he has to choose to see his church as a place of growth and a source of joy, to learn to see God at work there again.

Stay or Go?

There are only two healthy choices when it comes to our relationship with a church or ministry. One, we stay in that ministry, fully engaged in its vision and loving everyone involved. Two, we leave to find a place where we can be fully engaged in the mission and vision and love everyone involved. Either choice is good. But too many of us believe there are also choices three and four. Three, we stay but hate it, constantly complaining and feeling unhappy with the vision (or lack of vision) of the leaders and even ourselves in that context. Or four, we leave angry, only to isolate ourselves and actually become less committed to God in the leaving.

I advocate staying and leaving. Stay if you can do it in a joyful, hopeful way. Stay if you can fully support the ministry and its leaders. If not, leave. But don't leave God or community or mission. These things make us who we are. They should be a part of our lives because they are rivers of living water and tributaries of God's grace for us.

I understand the frustration and the feeling, sitting in

church thinking *Doing nothing would be better than doing this.* I understand the spiritual boredom you feel, the sense of irrelevance. Your critique may be valid and your feelings fair, but to step out only to become less committed to the cause of Christ is to succumb to the hypocrisy that we so abhor. So stay or leave, but do both with a sense of following Jesus and loving his mission and his people.

Some of us don't feel a release from God to leave, but in every other way we are leavers. We aren't sure how to make the decision objectively, and if we stay we aren't sure how to do so with joy. If this is you, I have a couple of tips on how to make this important decision, and then, if you chose to stay, I have other tips on how to remain faithful in the midst of frustrations.

How to Make the Decision

Objectivity both in yourself and in the people who advise you is a rare commodity. Making any decision can be like walking through a labyrinth of personal motivations and social agendas. Deciding to stay or leave a church is no different. Some feel pressured to out of obligation. For those who have grown up in church, it can be difficult to believe that to stop going could be an act of faith or obedience to God. Church attendance is one of the pillars of Christian discipline that we're taught from the time we're children. Even nonbelievers can feel some social pressure to attend church at least once or twice a year (usually Easter and Christmas). It is as if our spirituality and commitment to God can be measured by our church attendance.

In college, I was part of a church in which the number of times you attended in a week was a merit badge used to signify your love for God. "They are at the church every time the doors open" was a common affirmation. So how can we just stop going? Our decision is clouded by the real social sense that we will be turning our back on God if we stop going to church.

On the other hand, we might feel some internal (or external) pressure to leave for reasons that are equally poor. Some of our disaffection has to do with real concerns about mission or community or leadership or faithfulness to the Bible. But others are more personal, more petty. If we're honest, we know there are some things we just don't like about the worship service or a leader. And those problems reflect more about our own sinfulness and brokenness than they do about the church.

So, how can we stay when we may feel we are just caving to the social pressure to do so? And how can we leave when we may feel we are just being juvenile or hypercritical? The answer is simple to say but hard to do: Follow Jesus.

Be open. The first step to making any hard decision, especially one clouded by mixed motives, is to agree that God may be calling you to do either thing. In fact, I find it a good exercise to imagine God calling me to the thing I don't expect. This is important because so much of our listening prayer is drowned out by the noise of our expectations.

To hear God tell us something, we have to believe that he might. If you don't believe that God calls people to leave churches, the chances are you won't hear him say that to you. If you're so frustrated and so set on leaving that you don't see how God might call you to stay, chances are you won't hear him say that to you either. You can see the problem.

Going into a decision prayerfully open is an expression of worship. It reminds your own soul that you belong to God and that he is free to lead you wherever he wants. If your ears aren't open, everything else I'm going to suggest will make little sense. If Jesus is Lord of your life, he can deploy you where he wants. That is the beginning and end of wisdom for us.

Pray. How many decisions do we make every day without asking God? We have developed profound habits of self-reliance. Because a decision to stay will affect us and others in so many significant ways, we have to take the time necessary to ask God what to do. We must persevere in prayer on something like this. It may take more than one sitting to hear God clearly. Pray for as long as it takes, and then listen for an answer.

Listen to the Word. Scripture is more than a rulebook or history; it's a living document that speaks to us not only about the events of the past but also about the experience of our "right now." I suggest that before you make a decision, read the Bible. Read as much as you can as a kind of companion to the decision-making process. Sometimes you will find a character who is wrestling with similar questions or facing similar fears. Or course, you will not find your exact situation in the Bible, but rather God will speak to you through his Word. By reading through Scripture, you open another door for God to speak to you.

Ask the kingdom question. So much of our lives and the decisions we fret over revolve around issues Jesus taught us not to focus on. How often have we fretted about things like what we will eat and what we will wear? "The pagans run after all these things," he said. He taught his friends to concern themselves with the kingdom, with its well-being, with the needs of the kingdom of God (see Matthew 6).

> *I find myself staring off in the distance wondering,* How much do the stage lights cost? If they just focused them or changed the gels would it make the presentation better? *Or* Could I skip next week's service because I paid my dues in boredom this week? *Or* Who are the new people there? Does the church look empty? *Criticizing it makes me feel I'm at least thinking on my own.*
>
> CRYSTAL

This is more than a Christian cliché. Seeking the kingdom is the spiritual measurement of all decisions. Before you can decide to stay or leave, you have to ask the question, "What is best for the kingdom?" It may well be that you're very effective in your current church. And although you're frustrated with the leadership or some of the direction of the church, you know you have a fruitful ministry leading something at the church or through relationships that you will not be able to find somewhere else. So to stay would be a greater benefit to the kingdom. On the other hand, you may feel confined and unable to lead or love people in the way you know you can or are called to. In this case, leaving in order to be released to serve others would be the better choice for the kingdom. Asking the kingdom question moves the center of gravity away from you to a more trustworthy place. We can trust the answer to the kingdom question, and in most cases we should act on it.

Seek counsel from kingdom-minded friends. Many of us are individualistic and at the same time deeply insecure people, so we often don't use counselors well. Some of us are tempted to abdicate the process of spiritual decision making to the most spiritual, trusted person we know, asking her what to do and then simply following her advice as if it were from God himself. The problem with that is twofold. First, that person may be wrong, and you will be responsible before God for your decisions, not her. Second, if a counselor is willing to be the one to make your decision for you, you need to look for another counselor. This one isn't as spiritual as you think. A good counselor or confidant will listen well to you, ask good questions that make you think about the work God is doing in you and the elements surrounding your decision, and ultimately invite you to make your own decision. If you have a tendency to abdicate responsibility, look for a counselor who will force you back into the process with God, so that you make a decision in response to him, not the counselor.

Others of us are tempted not to listen to anyone. We may not want to ask anyone. For those of us who lean toward self-reliance, it's important to find counselors who can help us to see what we do not and challenge our appraisal of things. The self-reliant have a habit of either neglecting outside counsel or choosing counselors who will agree with their previously formed conclusions. Both corrupt the process of hearing God.

Try also to find people to talk to who aren't personally connected to the decision to stay or leave. For instance, a friend who has already left will most likely encourage you to do as he has done. It's best to rely on trusted friends who love Jesus, who are committed to the kingdom, who are willing to try to be objective and who don't have anything to gain by you leaving or staying. These kinds of friends make the best counselors.

Act. The process of deciding to stay or leave is important, but once you have faithfully gone through it and feel called to one thing or the other, it's equally important to do it. Sometimes we simply avoid what we know we should do, leaving us in church purgatory. If you feel like a leaver and you genuinely go through this process and believe that God is calling you to stay, you have to see that calling as a renaissance of your life at that church. It's a new beginning for you and your relationship with your church. Commit again to that church and be prepared to serve, worship and love with joy.

Staying Well

Believe that this will be a source of life and joy for you. God does not call people into places that will harm them spiritually. The same can't be said for other kinds of harm, such as physical. Often God does call his most faithful people into a life of hardship for the cause of Christ, a fact that is mediated by the many promises to reward such people with comfort in the life to come and intimacy with him now. I'm not saying that if you stay it will all be like a dream come true. On the contrary, I expect that if you stay you will continue to face the same frustrations that made you contemplate leaving in the first place. However, if it's God who is leading you to stay and your desire is to obey him, you ought to love that choice, love his will.

What is the hope of every follower but to obey the leading of the Master? More than you want any one thing, you should want to love and remain faithful to Jesus. If that is the case, staying is fulfilling that metadesire. That alone should give you joy. No matter what relational frustrations or structure obstacles you will face, face them with a sense that God has called you there and you're being faithful to him. This will give you a deeper sense of satisfaction than getting your way. If you're going to stay, stay with joy.

Stick with it for a set period. Once you've settled the question and decided to stay, it's important that you be free from the tyranny of the question itself for a season. If you don't set this mental boundary, it's likely you'll find yourself quickly reverting to being disconcerted, wondering all over again, *Why am I here?* As part of your decision process, you should set a time period in which you will not broach the subject again. One to two years seems reasonable to me, but let God lead you in that as well. This will free you to invest in the church and relationships, to bear with its weaknesses and to know that this is your church and that you're not going anywhere. Once that period has expired, you can again ask God about your place in the church. But until that time, you're free to focus your mental energy on productive kingdom activity.

Honor the leaders you're under. Much of what makes us frustrated about church is its leadership (or lack of leadership). Some of this critique is fair. Yet so much of what happens in a church is beyond the control or gifting of its leaders, and no church can survive without a healthy diet of grace for them. Because we see churches as divine institutions, we often are less tolerant of mistakes and choices with which we don't agree. However, the opposite should be true. Because the church is God's idea, it should be governed by his character, of which love and forgiveness are tantamount.

If you make the choice to stay at a church, you need to acknowledge that you're making the parallel choice to be submitted to the spiritual authority of that church. If you can't do this with confidence, don't stay. If you stay but undermine the authority or initiative of the leaders, your staying will be destructive and bad for the kingdom.

If you stay, honor your leaders. Honor does not mean you do everything they say. You're still responsible to follow Jesus. But honor means to speak well of them whenever they are mentioned. Honoring means to hold them in high regard in your heart, to pray for them and to wish well for them. Honor does not mean regarding them as perfect or holding back your concerns from them, but it does mean talking to them—and not anyone else—about your concerns.

Look for ways in, not ways out. If you choose to stay at a church where you have struggled, you have to know that God has called you there so that you can stay in a way that is constructive, hopeful and affirming. If Jesus has called you to stay, this is your community, and community is built by looking for ways in, not looking for ways out. Chances are, whatever it was that frustrated you about the church in the first place isn't going to change. So you will have to be the one who changes relative to that frustration. This means finding reasons to love and invest in that congregation. It means looking for the best in them.

This can be illustrated by romantic relationships. When a couple decides to marry, it's amazing how positive they can be about each other. These are people who have flaws—real, rough, ugly flaws. But people who want to marry don't focus on those things. They may admit certain flaws in each other, but those things are just not as significant to them. They see all the things about the other person that they love, that they want in their lives. Engagement is the quintessential posture of looking for ways in.

Fast-forward ten years. The same couple is now sitting in a counselor's office, talking about divorce. What changed? Those flaws they once overlooked are now all that they can see. When people want to marry, they focus on the things they love about each other and minimize their flaws. When people want to divorce, they focus on the things they don't like about each other and minimize what they used to love. If you choose to stay, you're choosing a relational commitment with something that is both flawed and lovable. If you choose to stay, you hold the key to your own survival and joy because you control what you focus on. Don't stay unless you're willing and can in good conscience overlook the flaws you see in your church. I'm not saying you have to pretend they're not there. I'm saying you have to emphasize the things that are noble, lovely and praiseworthy in your church instead.

We might want to stay to change the way things are. If this is your motivation, read on. In the next chapter we'll look at how your outlook on ushering in change can make or break your experience of staying.

10

STAYING FOR A CHANGE

*H*uman history has not been kind to prophets, to those who propose widespread change. Even the term *prophet* has become synonymous with a negative message. But it should not be so. Change implies error and imperfection, and although we all know that we are imperfect and need to change, we don't like to be reminded. Even if the prophet brings a message about the surpassing love of God for us and about our misunderstanding of that love, we rail against being told to wake up, to remember or to change.

As the first Christian martyr, Stephen understood that we always resist the prophets in our midst because they question our comfortable lives and they challenge the status quo. History is littered with great people who have been persecuted and killed for advocating change and for criticizing the way things are. However, everyone who criticizes is not a prophet. Prophetic and critical are far from being the same thing. Before we talk about change and how to effect it, it seems prudent to explore that distinction.

Are You a Prophet?

The prophet's message comes from God, is tested by God's Word and is communicated in love. There really aren't that many themes to prophecy. A survey of Old and New Testament prophets reveals that they were mostly calling for the same things: repentance, turning away from idols, doing justice, taking care of the poor. One way you can know if what you're feeling or saying is prophetic is to measure it against the history of prophecy; very few of us are called to tear down systems, and the life of a true prophet is often one of isolation, loneliness and pain. If you're not up for that, you're probably not called to be a true prophet.

The call to be that kind of person is something you discover only in a deeply real conversation with God. It isn't something you can get from a book. So, for everyone else, there's a less arduous route to smaller but significant change.

Being Prophetic

In the same way that each of us is called to share the gospel, to speak up for the weak, to live the life of an activist or an evangelist, we are called to be prophetic—to live a prophetic life. The mystique surrounding this word has only served to alienate everyday believers from what should be an accessible, albeit supernatural, expression of our very real connection to God. Every time we share Scripture with a friend, we are prophesying. Prophecy in its most understandable form is just speaking for God. On that level, even nonbelievers are capable of prophecy.

On another level, we might read another very specific Scripture to a friend at just the right time and in just the right way. This too is prophecy, but at an even more acute level. And occasionally we will even share a thought or impression that's biblical, in that it's consistent with the Bible, but original in its construct and context. This too can be prophecy, a way that God speaks to and through his people. I'm convinced that prophetic words should be a part of everyday Christianity. In humility, acknowledging always that we could be wrong, we should be prophesying to each other regularly. Having said that, it has to be clear that the error of false prophecy is also possible. But that's no reason to avoid attempting to discern the voice of God for the circumstances we find ourselves in.

For as long as I've done ministry, I've prayed one very simple prayer: *God, please don't let my sins be held against the people I serve.* I think I've always had an unresolved fear that my pride or selfish ambition related to the success of whatever ministry I was doing would be so egregious that God would have no choice but to hold back success from the endeavor. Maybe no one would know why, but in the end it would be God saying, "I can't bless this thing, Brian, because you're too proud and only failure will save you." While I don't rule that out on a personal level, I think that God has shown me over the years that he will bless what is submitted to him because he loves all involved and, perhaps more important, because there is a world to be reached, a world the needs to hear, and he will even use broken vessels because his motivation is so strong.

God is not going to silence his voice because we have misspoken. He is eager to be heard, and like other kinds of failure, false prophecy is forgivable. Like all sin, it is to be militantly feared and reviled in ourselves but treated with grace and understanding in others. Just as I can't let the fear of pride keep me from attempting great deeds for God, so our fear of false prophecy can't keep us from trying to hear and represent the voice of God in the world. The "testimony of Jesus is the spirit of prophecy" and presenting the gospel itself is the quintessential prophetic utterance (see Revelation 19:10).

Knowing God's Heart

Prophecy does not have to be negative. I once asked a group of my staff some simple questions: Is God happy with the human race? What about the church? When God looks at his people, is he pleased with them? Or is he disappointed? These are questions about which I've vacillated in the ten years since I first asked them. There are days when I feel connected to the heart of God for the poor, the violated, the abused and the forgotten, and I rage. But it isn't the kind of rage that comes from ego or self-interest. It's deeply spiritual and deeply honest. It's on these days, spent among the poor of the earth or remembering them in my heart, that I know God is not pleased. I know that the cries of the afflicted that rise to the throne of God day and night are indeed heard, and the promise of vengeance is the clear reply from the compassionate and powerful heart of God. On these days, I sense that God's anger burns against the child killers, the slaveholders and the frustrated megalomaniacs who make the weakest parts of humanity their theater of power. Yet on other days I sense the affection of God for me in such a way that I know it applies to a great sinner. I see in Scripture a God who loves the outcast, who sees epic failure and responds with mercy and tenderness. I find this reaction harder to understand, but I know it also represents the truth about God that no human being, no matter how despised or despicable, is beyond the love of God. On the contrary, that love seeks and saves those very people.

So which is truer than the other: God's anger or God's compassion? Or are they both true equally? How can that be? I still don't know the answer. I'm not entirely sure which one outweighs the other or how they intermingle in the mind and heart of God. But I know that both are true at some level. Scripture makes that clear. So prophecy and any call to change has to embody both of these realities.

Understanding Biblical Paradox

In his fascinating book *Sin, Pride & Self-Acceptance,* Terry Cooper explores the basic elements of human sin and discusses two apparently contradictory positions. The first is the Augustinian position that sin is rooted in pride, that all our rebellion is because we believe we are better or more than God. Our mistake is that we overestimate ourselves and underestimate God. The other position can be called Freudian, in that it makes the argument that all human sin is rooted in insecurity, that is, we underestimate the love of God and overestimate our inadequacies. Which is the core message human beings need to hear in order to be released from the bondage and cycle of sin? Is it that we are failures awaiting the judgment of God or that we are loved and awaiting the mercy of God?

It's hard not to take Augustine's side over Freud's, but progenitors aside, is it not a provocative question? What does the human heart more need to hear—encouragement or correction? Which produces the greater impact? It's his kindness that leads us to repentance, but it's still repentance that's needed, the acknowledgment that we are failures and that the wages of sin is death.

Maybe all people are not basically the same. And maybe we have to be faithful to the message no matter the impact. Again, the message of the cross is an offense to some and life to others. We have to call for change in a way that reflects the paradox of God's revealed mind on whatever we talk about. If I'm calling for change, I have a responsibility to first understand how God is pleased with the people and program that I'm talking about. If I hope to see a church change, I can't begin until I have a deep awareness of God's fair and merciful heart toward that church.

Perhaps part of our problem with being prophetic when it comes to the church is that we find ourselves incapable of holding these things in tension. Either we become convinced God is fed up with the blatant sin of a leader or a church and then write them off (passing judgment), or we realize God is merciful and decide that we ought not judge anyone so we abdicate our responsibility to decry sin or evil in all its forms in every place we find it. We simply can't ignore either.

Seeing God, understanding who he really is and in turn how to worship and to imitate him, will necessarily mean the embrace of paradox itself and the coalescence of this idea into our call for change. A paradox is defined as an apparent contradiction. That is, two ideas that seem incompatible at first glance but, when taken together, become the revelation of a new idea. When two things seem irreconcilable, their reconciliation illuminates a deeper truth. Paradox is the offer of a truer expression than what can be understood in a single idea alone.

On an intuitive level, we understand this to be true even if we have never given it words. Is God not a healer *and* a warrior? If we understand God as only one, does it not diminish him? And if we understand him as both on separate occasions, never looking to reconcile the revelations, does it not lead to confusion or religious prescriptivism? But if taken together, at the same time, does it not offer a deeper, more profound illumination of the perfection and beauty of God?

Paradox expands our understanding of God to infinite extremes. It refuses to confine God to any point on any continuum. God is both a prophet *and* a counselor. Mother *and* father. Master *and* friend. Infinite *and* personal. Inscrutable *and* knowable. Fearsome *and* winsome. In Jesus we see God as both God *and* man. In trinitarian theology we see God as both one and three. How is that possible? What has been called a mystery could also be called a paradox. God is both an individual *and* a community. In the revelation of God as both, we stand to grasp the way we must go, the destiny of the remaking of our own souls. God is at work, conforming us to the likeness of his Son. But what is that likeness?

True humility is possible only in the assertion of paradox. We have to understand the gospel, and even virtue itself, as a call to paradox and the embrace of not only what we are not but the challenge of the whole. Where we see dichotomy, we have to understand the infinite nature of God and the perfection of the Son. The inner life of the kingdom is best expressed in paradox, which keeps us humble, learning and longing for more of God and our own maturation. The discipline is to see the world and the work of God in these terms and to embrace the totality of the work of God in and around us. The world and its maker aren't confined by the certitudes of our opinions and dogmas. Being sure of a thing does not make it so. We are now and have always been in need of the standard of God's Word and the humility to rightly divide it.

Some of us are working on the streets of Manila with women caught in the snares of prostitution, and rage fills my belly. I want to exact a price from the bar owners, the pimps, the absentee fathers and brothers who all contribute to the web of broken virtue and clouded humanity. I burn. Even at night, I find myself, as a man and a father and a brother—and even as a Christ-follower—fantasying ways to make someone pay for such a system that uses women and girls for inhuman satiation. I want to get involved; I want to make someone feel the fury of my fear, the deepest fear I have: that I am inconsequential and powerless in a world of sin and hatred.

Why do I rage? Why can I not see that the bar owners and the pimps and the customers are all sinners like me? That they are, as I am, the object of both God's wrath and his intervening mercy? I would make them pay. But who will make me pay? What I really lack is power. What can I really do? What I fear is not that God is not just, that he will not be able to sort it all out, but that I'm of no use to him.

Paradox does not allow me to stay where I am. In paradox my rage is both right and wrong. God too is furious with the abuse of such a system, but he is also still extending mercy to all involved. Paradox does not condemn me but forces me to see the other way. The character of God is both my vindication and my discipline. Am I wrong to rage? No. And yes. The point is that my indignation may be righteous, but it is incomplete, inadequate. And paradox both exposes this reality and begs the deeper question: why can I see only one side? It uncovers the immaturity, the imperfection, the incompletion of my discipleship. I am, at once, like God and not like God.

Questions drive a theology of paradox because we are left to appreciate the work God has already done in us but also to ask what is left to be done. John writes, "If we confess our sins, he is faithful and just and will forgive us our sins and purify us from all unrighteousness" (1 John 1:9). He is faithful and just . . . he will forgive us. Even in that sentiment, John strikes the paradox. When we confess we have failed, God is both faithful (to forgive) and just (to punish). In our confession we remember the paradoxical character of God and the gospel of the kingdom. He does not just love; he also exacts justice. He is not only just; he is also merciful. At the same time, Paul writes of that process: "He who began a good work in you will carry it on to completion until the day of Christ Jesus" (Philippians 1:6). The paradox of his perfect character is what will be completed in me one day. He will finish the work in us to bring us both to understand that about him and to become like him ourselves.

But some things are just wrong. Period. So we tell ourselves. But it's God who is faithful and just. He will finish the work he has begun. What is that work? We have to ask on the streets, how can we can be agents of God's love? How can we offer what has been offered to us? Am I really following Jesus if the only people I offer grace to are the victims? Are not the victimizers also sinners in need of redemption? And if I see one pimp come to repentance, do I not also see women set free? When salvation comes to Zacchaeus (the sinner), aren't a dozen people who have been cheated rejoicing at his repentance? Isn't God's plan for redemption a plan to save the whole world? Aren't these slum racketeers also poor? These are the questions that a theology of paradox begs in me. For another, the questions might flow from a different origin. The theology of paradox embraces both a theology of protest and a theology of forgiveness. What ideology can boast such simple complexity?

Does that discount my rage? By no means! Here I find the secret of God, and I can't help but acknowledge that as the heavens are higher than the earth, so are his ways higher than my ways and his thoughts than mine. I'm moved to worship, because I realize that in his infinite capacity he sees all these injustices, and he rages and loves at the same time. This is our God. He sees evil and, rather than rain down fire from heaven on a creation that has made a despicable desecration of all his gifts, he stays his hand. God gave us beauty and color and virtue and the canvas of community, and we have smeared profanities and hatred into the fabric of his world. We are infidels. We are blasphemers. We are, all of us, God haters, criminals and perverts.

And we are the objects of his unfailing love. We, of all the things that he has created, are the expression of his greatest power: the power to redeem, to bring life from death and light from darkness, to bring love from hatred and hope from futility. This is our God. Who will not worship him? Who will not break before such mighty conviction, such loving fortitude? Who is so strong? Who is so incalculably great? Paradox drives us to the inevitable conclusion of the greatness of God. The mystery of Jesus is the mystery of the gospel of the kingdom, and the mystery of the gospel of the kingdom is the mystery of divine personality. We learn the kingdom's ways so that we can understand the king. "The mystery of Jesus," James Stewart wrote, "is the mystery of divine personality." On our quest to follow Jesus and to imitate God, we have to understand that behind every theological inquiry is the paradox of the perfect personality. He can't be understood by one idea. He can't be contained in our dogma. Wonder is found in the search for and respect of the tension in the paradox of God.

What does it mean then to walk in the steps of a God we know as a man and a man we worship as God? To know the unknowable? To follow a God we can't see but whom we have seen? What does it mean to follow Jesus, who can be known to us only in the tension of these paradoxes? We need to call for change in ourselves and in others. But we have to understand that things are never exactly as we appraise them. The tension between the need to change and the grace of God pulls both ways. It is both an affirmation of a prophetic call and a caution. Once we understand this, we will be more likely to communicate the true heart of God when we call for change.

Our Leaving Story

I was part of a large group of people who were all leaving churches at the same time. Some of them looked to me as a leader in the midst of this transition, likely because I always had been quick to talk about what I saw going wrong in the churches in our area. These critiques may have been fair and accurate, but they were only half of the story. When it came time to gather these people together, it dawned on me that we were creating a culture of deconstruction. We were all too eager to talk about what was wrong and were not as aware of or articulate on what was right.

Naively I assumed I could organize and lead these people into a new kind of community, a new kind of church that would not make the same mistakes, one that would make sense to them. The problem is that one of the primary similarities between us was that we all were critical, a characteristic that was not going to change just because we made a few changes. Many leavers are critical and self-confident. They have to be; there's very little support available to people leaving churches as an act of faithfulness to God. So this group in particular had to be sure of their grievances and also self-assured enough to follow through on them. They were both.

I loved this group. I loved the way they thought, what they hoped for and the potential I saw in them. Like other leavers, this group was amazingly missional and capable of so much when networked together and focused on something that mattered to God. But what of the culture of deconstructing? Who would be crazy enough to build something with a group of people whose main skill and interest is in taking things apart. I confess that I was not particularly aware of this dynamic then. Hindsight is 20/20.

But God was aware. Not being entirely sure why, I sensed that before we could do anything together, God was calling us into a season of prayer and intercession for the church and our city. I knew that we were not in the right place to build something and even that we were not right to be critical of something we did not truly love and had not labored for in prayer. So we committed ourselves to a year of prayer and intercession together for our city and for the church invisible. The result was that our love for the church in our city grew through intercession and our hubris shrank in the presence of God.

Out of that prayer gathering would be born the Underground Network and our attempt at a proactive approach to change. We decided that we would try to change our culture. We decided that for us to be prophetic meant that we would live our hopes and confine our criticism to ourselves. We wanted to be an alley to the rest of the church in our city, supporting others with prayer but working for change in our structure and character.

One nice thing about the church in the United States is that we learn from success. Churches don't change because people criticize them. In fact, it might be that criticism, especially from the outside, further entrenches churches in their error. The churches that are open to change will change because they see something that works and is transferable. We realized that raging against the church in our city was prophetic but not productive. God is calling us to be both. As Paul wrote, love always hopes. We have to live prophetically, calling through our prayers and actions for the kind of change we believe God is working toward. A prophetic life is what will bring about change.

Being prophetic means representing the truth about God as best we can within the limitations of our personality. This isn't simply a matter of saying two positive things before you say one negative. It's knowing what pleases God and saying it with as much conviction and passion as you would have when speaking about what does not please God.

Staying and Change

If you see yourself as an agent of change, chances are no one else will. The problem with ordinary people being prophets is that we have flaws too. Sometimes these flaws affect our prophecy. So when we are judging a situation and calling for change, our miscalculations or inadequate perspectives can betray the change we are so eager to bring about.

Do not change your goal. Even for the prophet, change isn't the goal. The goal is simply to present the need for change. The prophet is successful if she has faithfully communicated the heart of God, not if people change. Jeremiah was certainly not a less faithful prophet than Jonah, even though Jonah's initial message met with the greatest repentance. Success is in the transmission of the message, not in the response to it. Certainly we hope that our message will be received, but if we put too much weight on that, we will most likely stay very frustrated. God may be looking for some change from a group, but (and this is very obvious but also very important) we are not God. However, when we make changing a person or a group our goal, we are assuming his role, which isn't something I recommend! We rarely intend to play God, but when we set out to change, control or judge another man's servant, we are in danger of losing our connection to the God we are trying to represent.

Early in my marriage, this was something I did not understand. There were things about Monica that I just knew needed to change. I thought, since I was her husband and I was supposed to be a leader in my home, that any deficiency, no matter how small, in her spiritual life or character was a deficiency in me. I believed I needed to be relentless in my work to change those things.

For a long time, I thought our marriage was going just fine. Until one day Monica had simply had enough. She sat me down and explained how I was actually disempowering her by pointing out what I thought was wrong with her. She never disputed my analysis, just that my posture toward her was actually hurting her relationship with God, making change in those particular areas that much more inaccessible. It didn't happen overnight, but I learned a very important lesson, one that for the most part I've maintained since: Monica isn't mine to change. Once I let go of that responsibility, a huge burden was lifted from my shoulders. She felt freer to pursue God in those areas, and our relationship was tangibly better. Now I make it my responsibility to affirm her when I see her changing in response to God but to accept her in every other way, as she is.

This choice to love her as she is has had other interesting side effects. For instance, Monica is chronically uninterested in my deep theological thoughts. She falls asleep while I'm sharing some "profound" idea that I have. I used to resent it. I thought she should care about these things the way I do. And I argued that to be uninterested in these things was a weakness on her part. But when I decided to love Monica for who she is and not to work to make her someone else, I actually grew to love this characteristic. I've come to see what a gift she is to me precisely because she has never been impressed by any of my ideas or my ability to explain them. Others are, so I get more than my fair share of accolades. I don't need that from her. She simply isn't impressed by me in that way. She never has been. But she still loves me. She does not love me for my performance as a minister or thinker or leader. In fact, all of that kind of bores her. She just wants to be with me as I am. I would not suggest that as a posture for every spouse, but for me it is a gift, and I've come to appreciate it and her for that.

Monica is deeply spiritual and committed to Jesus in all the ways that matter. But she is different from me. Part of letting go of the need to change someone is coming to terms with the truth that people are different, and some of the things we think need to change in them are really more of a reflection of our own needs. Releasing that person or people from your control is an important first step in being used by God to effect change.

Good stayers build relationships with leaders to bless them and not to change them. I would suggest that you take some time to build a friendship with the leaders of your church. Don't do it to change them, but to be known to them and to know them in a personal way. As change agents, we tend to see all the flaws of our church as an extension of the pastor or church leadership. If we don't know them personally, we can be tempted to vilify them for everything that we see going wrong. This relational deficiency can lead to a dehumanizing of the leaders and shortsightedness in our appraisals of church dynamics.

Likewise, as you are living out your commitment to Jesus in new or different ways, those same leaders will be tempted to dehumanize and misunderstand you. Keeping a connection built on service and the commitment to bless that pastor will minimize the misunderstanding and allow you the best chance not only to survive in that church but even to gain a hearing for some of your ideas. Take this very seriously. If you try to live under the radar of the church and its leaders, living faithfully in the light of your commitments but otherwise just trying to go unnoticed, you have to ask yourself why you're staying at all. Chances are, if God has called you to stay it is because he wants you to live prophetically and to love and possibly even lead those leaders.

Treasure small movements and little breakthroughs. If you're going to make it in an environment that doesn't appreciate or reward your faith choices or vision for the future, you're going to have to be able to enjoy tiny amounts of change. For you, small movements have to be felt as seismic events. Because living faithfully to Jesus Christ among the people where he has placed you—not widespread change—is your goal, you can see any change as icing on the cake. Icing is something that cakes should have, and so you can not only hope for change but also expect it as you live your convictions with honesty, passion, love and humility. If you're able to marshal a small community, the criticism may outweigh the affirmation, but when people do see and are moved by your lives, you have to see just what a gift that is and celebrate it.

11

LIVING CHANGE

As a senior in college, I was often blinded by hubris. I can remember weighing my postcollege options. I knew I was called to ministry, and I'd been offered a scholarship to a seminary. It seemed like the best option. Yet my InterVarsity staff worker sat me down one afternoon to tell me he thought I should consider joining staff. I laughed.

This man was one of those rare Christlike leaders who did not lead out of ego or control. He quietly loved and led all of us toward a godly vision and developed a healthy missional community on campus, but we took all the credit. Even at that moment, he just smiled and asked me to think about it.

I didn't want to be on staff because I wanted to have more influence as a leader than I saw InterVarsity staff having. Their brand of leadership through service and strength through humility was unappealing from my immature outlook. When I was later invited to a staff-recruiting weekend, I didn't see the harm in going, so I said yes. Once there, I had two conversations that would change the direction of my life.

I can't remember the topic of the first conversation, with the InterVarsity area director for North and Central Florida, but I do remember how it turned. I said something about which he just smiled and said with love, honesty and a little bit of mirth, "Brian, you are just so arrogant." No one had ever said that to my face. I knew I had a pride problem, but to have someone just say it like that was, well, invigorating. I wasn't angry. On the contrary, I was so happy, I couldn't stop thinking about it—until later that night when another staff supervisor was listening to me talk about how this thing or that thing needed to change. He said, "Brian, you may be right in what you're saying, but *you* are not right. It's okay to tip over the apple cart from time to time, but a real follower of Jesus would stick around and help pick up the apples." It might seem like a strange reason to go into college ministry, but I knew then that I needed to be around these kind of people. People who could look me in the eye, call out my sin and love me toward growth. I knew I stood to learn more from men and women like that than I could ever learn from books.

I learned that night that the organizational humility and honesty of InterVarsity was just what I needed to become more like Jesus. I also learned that saying something needs to change does not make you Christlike. Helping to make change possible is Christlike. Can you imagine if God would have taken the posture I took toward broken systems? If he had simply shaken his fists at our incompetence to be righteous and hurled insults and judgments at us, yelling, Why can't you people get your act together? Yes, if we are going to overturn the proverbial apple carts at the churches we attend, we have to be equally committed to helping pick up the apples.

The Integrity Challenge

The trouble with staying is that we will feel caught between two worlds, frustrated by our inability to fully identify with either. On one hand is the temptation to capitulate to the status quo of the church we feel called to, not just living with the flaws but also giving up the fight for more and learning to accept the mediocrity of the church. Or even worse, forgetting what we once knew church could be. On the other hand is the temptation to stay physically but leave emotionally, to dismiss the church as incapable of change and shut our hearts to the leadership and the direction of the church. Living in-between can be very hard. But if you feel called to stay, you have to trust that God will allot the grace necessary for you to stay in a healthy way.

The first challenge is integrity. If you say you believe in something but don't do it, you lie. This simple truth often separates authentic (albeit flawed) Christianity from the hypocritical variety. Authentic Christianity can carry with it all kinds of mistakes and misapplications, but it will always carry with it a kind of power, because at the place that it's most important it is real and righteous. The question of truth that every nonbeliever asks is a question that permeates all of life, not just the intellectual, propositional kind of truth but the kind of truth that asks, Does this actually work? Someone may explain to me the principles behind CPR and I may well agree that these things are true, but I still want to know, Does it work? Have you ever seen it work? If my heart stops, will it help? Or if the heart of one of my children stops and I perform CPR, will I be able to save her? If the answer is no, then who cares?

We have to offer humanity a gospel that can transform, that has the power to change us. There simply is no other way to communicate that kind of gospel than to live a life that's being transformed. With all our flaws, the core truth of the gospel is most clearly articulated by our submission to live what we have heard. Our struggle to obey is what makes us authentic and our message true. When we accept the gospel but don't let it infiltrate the corners of our routines and assumptions, we aren't true and the gospel we proclaim is without power.

I say all that to make this simple point: You have to live what you believe. You can choose to stay only if you know that you have to live out the life of Jesus as you understand it and in the ways that are most important to you. Don't paint yourself into a spiritual or theological corner by having to choose between being true and being submitted to your local church. If you know that staying will mean that you can no longer be the kind of Christian you know you should be, you must leave. In many cases, it isn't that our churches don't allow us to be faithful to the way of Jesus, but only that we will have to do it alone. If this is the case, you may be able to stay.

For instance, if you believe that believers should actively share their faith, but your church does not agree and seldom does evangelism, you still may be able to stay. But know that if you do, you must double your commitment to evangelism and live it in spite of the current flowing against it. You have to build around you a countercultural community that will endorse your lifestyle of proclamation or else that virtue will surely die.

Or if you know that God has called you to care for the poor, but you are in a church that gives very little attention to the poor, you can stay only if you can find a way to live out that value in that church. It may well be that you will bring about change as you're faithfully loving the poor with a few people.

But the first question to ask is, can I do that? If you know that you don't have like-minded people to partner with in that cause and you know that the prospect of finding or influencing other church members to follow you and learn from you in that conviction is slim to nonexistent, you need to more seriously consider leaving.

Please believe me. I don't give that counsel to leave your local church lightly. Nor am I being cavalier when I suggest it. Yet I know that to stay in a church and not live in the light of the discipleship of the Master is to lose the sense of his presence. There is a fine line between inactivity and hypocrisy, and the former leads to the latter. Hypocrisy will mean the death of your soul, and for that reason, avoiding it is a higher priority than church attendance. If you can't follow Jesus in your church, it isn't the church for you anyway. So don't hesitate to leave. Your integrity is precious and can't be underestimated.

Countercultural Communities

For years I've wondered how to sustain radicalism. In working with college students and young professionals, I've seen great levels of commitment to extraordinary, uncommon ideals, and I've seen the sacrifice necessary to live those ideals in counter-cultural ways. But it doesn't ever seem to last. I can't say that this has been true in every case, but in too many it has. Young people who were completely sold out for the cause of Christ, whose lucid love for Jesus began to conjure hope for that revolution George Barna talks about, fade into a mediocre McLife. I catch up with them some years later, and they are positively pacified. It breaks my heart. I understand that some of what I'm seeing is stage-of-life priorities, but some is compromise too. And so I wonder, *How can radical choices be sustained?*

When I see the cultural current to have the new car, the nice house, the high-paying job, the vacation, the retirement plan, I start asking myself, "What's wrong with those things?" And maybe nothing is wrong with them. What is wrong is that no one seems to be asking if they're wrong. The thing that scares me is when my culture makes moral and material choices for me, when the current of popular culture, Christian or otherwise, operates as a moral consensus unchecked by prayer, Scripture or the kingdom question. I want to be able to say no or yes to any decision because I've weighed it in the light of the kingdom of God. When you choose against culture, they call you a radical. But who can survive as a radical in a sea of moderates?

By nature, we are predisposed to fit in. When given the option between standing out negatively or conforming, we will conform. Certainly that is a good characteristic when the majority is right. But what about when it's not? The only way to sustain radical, unconventional choices is to make them conventional somewhere. Where I've seen real countercultural behavior, it exists because people have surrounded themselves with another kind of community, creating a new convention. In other words, people have to conform, so we need to create communities that allow us to conform to Jesus and his way. Strong, biblical, Jesus-following communities are the key to sustaining countercultural behavior.

The same is true in your church. For example, if you hope to maintain a value and practice of material simplicity in a church of upper-class congregants, you're going to struggle. The solution is to generate a small community around you that shares your value for simplicity. If you can find those people within the church (they may be there; you are, after all), try to do that. But if you can't find them there, find them somewhere. Surrounding yourself with people who affirm your conviction is the only thing that will preserve it.

The Paradox of Staying

I believe that change is possible only if an actual alternative is preserved. Yet we can't bring about change if we simply stand outside a system and call for change as an alternative. In other words, you need to be an insider to effect real change, but being on the inside will compromise your vision for change.

People live in one community at a time. Are we creating alternatives for the world or are we, as members of the world, trying to change it? Most certainly both. We create alternatives when we are powerless and we find that changing is only possible if we live that change first. Finding a few people who have a similar vision of the church and life together can be the difference between authenticity and falsehood.

The incarnation is an expression of this paradox. Jesus, who lived a perfect life, offers us an alternative to the life of sin and rebellion that we all have chosen. God, in Christ, critiques our way of living and dying with another way, but he displays that revolutionary option by becoming like us. His choice to endure but not succumb, to be offered the lie of every temptation that tantalizes us and even to taste the fruit of our sin—death forever—made him one of us, the truest insider. He now calls for change as one who knows, and he marshals an army of people who need someone who is like them.

Jesus became like us to change us while, at the same time, maintaining a community with the Father and the Spirit that's nothing like us. He is both transcendent and intimate, revealing not only the formula for real leadership and effecting positive change but also the character of God. When Jesus taught his disciples to pray, he told them to refer to God as "Our Father" in heaven. He understood the paradox of his own incarnation and that he was revealing something true about God. He is our Father, one who is close and personal, who can be asked for things and who loves us. Yet he is also in heaven, transcendent and as far away from us as we can imagine. The early church wrestled with the implication of this seemingly impossible paradox, torn between the spiritual or supernatural and the physical or natural truth about Jesus. But the church eventually settled in the beauty and logic of the paradox.

Change is best engineered by a transcendent insider. Jesus lived on the threshold between heaven and earth. He brought the alternative of heaven into the realities of earth. He was the consummate idealist; he knew the reality of the perfection of heaven, what Plato called the ideal forms of all things. Yet Jesus stepped from that ideal world into the brokenness of our world. Never compromising his vision of what he knew was possible in heaven, he took flesh and pitched his tent in the desert of human suffering.

If we are to effect change, it will have to be as independent communities connected to the rest of the church. The recent trend for radical communities to cloister themselves away in neomonastic isolation may seem novel, but it will not create lasting change in the church unless the ideas and passion behind such sacrifice and community formation become a part of the dialogue of the church at large. My community represents a part of this new trend. Certainly we understand the lure of an isolated, self-defining Christianity. We understand what it's like to be misunderstood, to be called a commune, to be thought of as hippies because we try to live simply or live in a multifamily household. But our vision of community isn't perfect, and it needs to be offered as an imperfect gift to the body of Christ. We have to find a way to become the church as people know it, while never ceasing to be the church as we know it.

Church as an Ideal and as a Group

Throughout this book, I've used the word *church* to mean the thing that we are leaving, the local expression that is so frail and imperfect and even at times deviant. Yet I'm also using the same word to signify the church we hope for, the church as an ideal. I've intentionally left this ambiguity intact, leaving the term to mean both things because this is the reality of church.

This lack of clarity forces us to ask ecclesiological questions every time the word is used, to think about the context of the term and to discern what it is. The painful reality is that the church is both the ideal we love and long for and the awkward group of people meeting once a week in hallowed halls and middle school cafeterias. Church is a place where the leaders of God's people bear great spiritual authority and also a place where people lie and tell tall tales just to get your money. Just as Jesus said, "Many will come in my name, claiming, 'I am the Christ'" (Matthew 24:5), many come in the name of the church, saying we are it. But that does not make it so.

Knowing that there will be imposters doesn't inspire Jesus to change his name. What good would that do? They would use the new name. But it does inspire him to warn his followers to watch out. In the same way, we have to be vigilant when it comes to the idea and practice of church. We have to hold it as a concept and as a practice in the highest regard, while at the same time being willing and able to decry its false manifestations, when those manifestations are within other people and when they are within ourselves.

Uncommon Commitment Needed

Following Jesus takes uncommon commitment. Vision, integrity, countercultural community, uncommon commitment—these are the seeds of our revolution. If you're not deeply committed to your cause and your assignment, you have little chance of surviving spiritually in a place that doesn't affirm you. The trick to spiritual commitment is making the connection between the platitudes we pray and the life we actually live. I'm often frustrated with myself and others when we say we are willing to forsake all for Jesus and then, when following Jesus becomes hard (as he promised it would), our spiritual resolve is nonexistent.

Recently I was talking to a committed Christian about a decision before him. The kingdom choice seemed obvious to me, but he was not even considering it. I asked him what sense he had from God, what he thought the Lord wanted. He was instantly annoyed. His furrowed brow and twisted expression communicated to me that my question was out of bounds, almost as if he were saying to me, "What does that have to do with anything?" or "Oh nice, Brian, thanks for bringing up God." It was as if my mention of Jesus and his commitment to Jesus were an inconvenience to making the decision he wanted to make. Bringing Jesus up was a spiritual low blow.

I have a friend who has a gift for reminding people of the prayers they have prayed and the commitments they have made. He's notorious for asking penetrating spiritual questions at odd times and in socially surface moments. It's entertaining to watch him interact with Christians, and it's always awkward. He reminds me just how unwelcome Jesus is in too many of our conversations. We are too often committed to Jesus and his kingdom in word only; we speak it only in certain contexts and when we have our spiritual face on.

This kind of Christianity tries me. I have to admit that I don't want anything to do with it. Neither did the apostle Paul or James.

The faith we have to quietly yet boldly live in our churches is one of love, and love inspires the greatest kinds of sacrifice. We have to be so committed to the gospel of the kingdom that we are willing to pay whatever price we have to, to see that the kingdom expands and God is honored.

Staying is not easier. In some ways it's harder. But it isn't a matter of easy or hard. The things of the kingdom aren't worth comparing with words like *easy* and *hard*. Whatever God has called you to is going to be hard. If you stay, it will require restraint and understanding and patience beyond what you think you possess. If you leave, it will require other virtues. In each case, if you're where God has called you, you can be sure that it will be both difficult and rewarding. This is the way of the kingdom. It is a pearl of great price, so that a man sells all that he has to buy it.

Staying is not easier. It will require you selling all that you have to possess instead the kingdom in that congregation.

George Barna's recently published book *Revolution* deals at length with the leavers phenomenon. He offers what could be called a sympathetic outsider's analysis of the somewhat shocking trend of committed Christians finding ways to serve God without going to church. The book title and running theme of revolution speaks to the heart of leavers' deeper hopes. My friends and I do believe that a revolution is possible, but we aren't revolutionaries. Not that I mind thinking about a revolution and all that that means. On the contrary, I believe something like a revolution is needed. It's simply that I see the trend toward leaving as something we're doing because we simply don't know what else to do.

I want to see a revolution, but this isn't it. We are too disorganized, we are leaving without vision for something more, and too many of us are simply groping blindly for spiritual health as leavers. It's all we can do to simply survive the leaving. While I'm flattered and encouraged by someone like Barna using such strong words for our choices, I have to believe that there is so much more that is possible. Revolutionary change may be on the horizon, but we aren't there yet.

Wolfgang Simson has said that a rebel is just a radical without his Father's heart. I agree. Some leavers are simply rebelling against what they know church should not be, but they aren't working to develop church into what it can be. A new, web-based church called the Revolution Church, led by Jay Bakker (Jim and Tammy Faye's son), is a good example. They recently started a marketing campaign that reads, "As Christians, we are sorry for being self-righteous judgmental bastards. Revolution. An online church for people who have given up on church." This church has the revolutionary urge, and I admire their creativity, honesty and commitment to their mission target. Yet while this generation of believers sees that something needs to change, and they are beginning to organize, much of what they are forming is really just a reaction to what they don't like. They like the idea of revolution, not reformation, because revolution connotes a displacement of the current system and all its tributaries.

However, for the student of historical revolutions, the prospect of overthrow of one power structure for a brand-new one isn't all that promising. The caution for young movements (like my own organization) is that we have to show enough humility and wisdom in our youth to see that we can't define our revolution as simply the opposite of the status quo. We have to be more sophisticated. Please don't misunderstand me. I'm still looking for revolutionary change, but that change has to be more than rock music and welcoming an alternative crowd. We have to do that, but if we exchange one kind of uniformity for another, what have we really changed? Would not a revolution of inclusion look more like multiethnic community with all economic and social classes involved? This, I'm afraid, is a tall order, but one worth leaving for. We have to avoid the temptation to define our mission by what we are not going to do and who we are not going to be. We need clarity about our unique place and what we are called to build.

This final section is an attempt to talk about the revolutionary possibilities of leaving. And I emphasize *possibilities*. They can be realized only through the grace of God and some determination and vision on our part. But leaving can fuel a new kind of church that stands on the foundations laid by the current church and the wisdom of the ancient church—not on its rubble. I hope we can leave in a way that reforms us into the churches and communities we hope for.

12

LEAVING WELL

*C*hoosing to leave should be an apostolic movement. We should never leave angry (although we often do) but leave with a sense of purpose and hope, as a response to God's initiative. In other words, it isn't so much that we are leaving as we are being sent.

Acknowledge God's Leading

We may have myriad reasons for leaving, but the sense that we are following God's leading is by far the most important. In the end, it's the sole reason to leave—or do anything at all. In matters that are disputable and not moral in nature, Paul instructed the Romans, "Everything that does not come from faith is sin" (Romans 14:23). Leaving has to be done in faith.

It may still seem strange to say or hear, but leaving has to be a response to faithfully following Jesus. As we leave, the primacy of this reason has to be what we acknowledge as we explain ourselves to others. Sometimes we feel reticent to attribute our decisions to God, and in this case it may seem socially simpler or more natural to point to one of our other reasons for leaving. But exposing the church by referring to these reasons draws attention to the church's flaws (as you see them). Disparaging the church or its leaders as we leave only casts a shadow on what is already going to be a difficult decision for some people to understand. It's best to acknowledge that your departure isn't due to any particular deficiency in the church but rather to God's leading in your life. In this way, you turn a potentially destructive conversation into an opportunity for discipleship. It will be strange for some of our friends or family to hear that we sense God leading us to leave, but our testimony to that option opens them up to the possibility.

Stay Positive

As we share our story, it may not be possible to confine our exit motivation to God's leading alone. Giving God credit for the decision moves us closer to a wholesome, edifying explanation for our leaving. Practicing the discipline of Philippians 4:8 is a good rule: "Finally, brothers, whatever is true, whatever is noble, whatever is right, whatever is pure, whatever is lovely, whatever is admirable—if anything is excellent or praiseworthy—think about such things."

Find ways to talk about what is strong or healthy in the church. Even if you think there's nothing, in almost every case that isn't true. Unless the church has been involved in something criminal, the best exit is a gracious one. God is working even in the darkest places. Try to pay attention to him and his work in the church.

I'm not suggesting that you be dishonest. You'll need to share your heartbreak and frustration over what has been done to you or left undone. Do this only with mature people close to you. Knowing that leaving will speed your healing in those areas, try not to hurt anyone else while you nurse those wounds. In fact, staying positive and taking the high ground will never vindicate you, but it will leave you in the hands of the One who can. Again in his letter to the Romans, who were struggling through divisive controversy, Paul wrote, "Do not overcome evil by evil, but overcome evil with good" (12:21). Leaving with honor on your lips is the best practice for you and for the church.

Of all these recommendations, this was probably the hardest for me. Maybe it's because I'm predisposed to be negative, I don't know, but consciously I've seen some churches I've been a part of as sinking ships. I wanted to warn people, as an act of love and service, to get off while they could. I was tempted to see my appraisal as comprehensive.

In one case, I saw the coming demise of the church's leadership. I saw one poor decision after another being made. I went to the pastor, who was a close friend, and challenged him to step out of certain roles that he was not equipped to manage but stay in leadership and stay connected to the body. He did not. Within six months, he packed up and left, overwhelmed by the tasks he could not manage. The church was left abandoned and leaking from all the holes in the ship. I had already felt called to leave too, so the decision did not affect me directly, but I grieved for the congregation. I watched as the leadership void became overloaded with power players, and I wished I'd warned more people. I wished I could have spared more people from the desperate state they were now in.

But what does my need to tell people my negative appraisal really mean? How can I trust God to lead me and reveal to me what he wants for me but not trust him to do the same for others? Am I really the only person who can hear God clearly on something like this?

I love the heart of the apostle Paul, who wrote in the close of his letter to the Romans, "I myself am convinced, my brothers, that you yourselves are full of goodness, complete in knowledge and competent to instruct one another" (15:14). He said this to the same people he had spent the previous fourteen chapters teaching and rebuking. He went on to write, "I have written . . . to remind you." In other words, you already know all the things I've said. I'm just writing to remind you, because you're made "competent" by the grace and presence of the Holy Spirit.

Reading the rest of the chapter reveals Paul's motivation. He was trying to help them to understand why he had not come to them, why he might still fail to make it to visit the church in the most important city in the world. Spain was calling. Paul was called and sent by Jesus Christ to be an apostle to the Gentiles (the whole unbelieving world), and he simply didn't have time to control or micromanage those Roman Christians.

I'm convinced that Paul's apostolic instincts and ambitions resulted in an unexpected and excellent side effect: he was too busy on his mission to worry about controlling Christians. He explained his vision for reaching people who don't know instead of micromanaging people who do:

> It has always been my ambition to preach the gospel where Christ was not known, so that I would not be building on someone else's foundation. Rather, as it is written:
>
> "Those who were not told about him will see,
> and those who have not heard will understand."
>
> This is why I have often been hindered from coming to you. (Romans 15:20-22)

We have to relinquish control of the world, which only God should control. Control fixation is destructive everywhere, but in the church it's deadly. We have to employ radical trust in the God who says he will build and purify his own church in his own way and in his own time. We have to get busy being what we know God has called us to for the sake of his kingdom and his mission. Everything else is a distraction.

So then how can we talk about what we are doing at all? How can we be honest about our leaving? If everything in the church we are leaving is so great, why would God be calling us to leave?

Talk About the Future

We need a way of sharing with people our motivation to leave, but we have to discipline ourselves to share it in terms of our hope, our vision and our disaffection. I will give you an example. Let's say you're leaving a church in part because of an unhealthy leader, who is power hungry and dominates every facet of the church life. I attended a church where the pastor preached every week and was also the music and worship leader and had to have every decision go through him. Maybe you're convinced this is producing bad fruit, and it's time for you to leave. How do you talk about it without disparaging that leader? Try using a vision for something different. Someone might ask, "Why are you leaving?" You could say, "Because this pastor acts like he's God. His dominating leadership is unbiblical and wrong." Or you could say, "I'm leaving because I'm excited about the possibility of being a part of a church that shares leadership and where everyone in the congregation can use their gifts."

David was a leaver. He was trapped under the oppressive and heartless leadership of King Saul. David knew he was called ultimately to lead Israel in a different way; he knew he was even called and chosen by God to do that. But when given the opportunity, while Saul was still in authority, David refused to throw his spear at him. With all his friends cheering him on, David showed a Jesus-like resolve to respect the king for as long as he was king. That didn't mean that David stuck around to be killed himself. On the contrary, he journeyed in the wilderness with his community, fighting evil where they could and worshiping God as best they knew how, until the day would come when God would give David a chance to lead.

Like David, we can also refuse to throw spears at the bad leader. From a human perspective, Saul could have used a good spear in the back. But from God's perspective, David was being groomed to be a great king, and great leaders are born from respect of authority and submission. Great leaders know how to follow. Great leaders don't tear down other leaders, *especially* when they're wrong.

Instead we have to talk about our hope and our vision for what the church can be. We can't remain silent. You may think there's very little difference, that the person listening will still interpret that positive remark as a slight against the current pastor. But that's not necessarily true. People will read a critique into your remark only if they already see that flaw. In such a case, you're not tearing the pastor down, but only affirming what they too hope for in their hearts. Those people who don't see that leader in that light will likely miss the critique. They'll simply understand that you're looking for something different. Not necessarily better, just different.

> *The majority of the people I hang out with in the past few years are not Christians, and church is just not a priority or even an interest. So while I could be spending time building a relationship with them and discussing Jesus with them in a more natural and less forced setting, I am helping to plan programs for churches that are trying to attract people.*
>
> TODD

Plan to Finish Well

Making up your mind to leave and leaving should rarely happen simultaneously. Once you know that God is calling you to leave, you're at the beginning of your next assignment: finishing well. Just knowing that you're released to leave can bring a certain freedom and excitement about the future. That excitement can distract us from finishing well, or it can be used to enjoy the final weeks at a place that has many things to appreciate and bless.

I suggest you make an exit plan. Think through who needs

to be told and in what order. Some people will be able to hear about your leaving through the grapevine and suffer no offense, but certainly there are people who will want to hear it from you and need you to explain it to them personally.

I generally believe that, outside your most intimate community, it's important to talk with the church's leaders first. A humble, thankful, yet resolved posture with a pastor or leader can be the first important step in finishing well. Be gracious and loving, but stand your ground and be honest about why you failed to thrive in the church. Your loving honesty can be a great gift to that leader. Try not to expect too much; simply make it your goal to honor him by explaining why you're feeling called to leave. This is the appropriate place to express your frustration in a constructive way. It may be one of the only places, because this is the person who needs to know and who, in many cases, can make changes.

Further, that conversation can help you to map out the rest of your exit strategy. I suggest you ask your pastor or elder how she would like you to leave and in what ways you can serve the church as you depart. Be willing to take as many weeks as necessary to satisfy those leaders without being dissuaded from leaving. Taking even six months to leave well can be worth it for you. It will give you a sense of closure and peace of mind as you know that you not only did what Jesus was leading you to do but also did it in a way Jesus wanted you to. We are capable of doing the right thing in the wrong way. Planning well can prevent that outcome.

Replace Yourself

Part of leaving with integrity is to replace yourself. After you have communicated with all the right people about your intentions to leave, you have to think through any responsibility (formal or otherwise) you have at the church. If you hold a leadership role or serve in some unique way that will be missed, leaving well may mean finding someone to take over that role. It could be that you're a greeter at your weekly service, a member of a committee or a Sunday school teacher. Even if you're not directly responsible for finding people to fill those roles, it's an act of forethought and care for the church to think through who could replace you and even to have a conversation with that person about taking your role when you leave. When we fail to consider something this obvious, we communicate a lack of concern for the fellowship of God's people.

Say Thank You

Again, part of leaving well is honoring and celebrating the praiseworthy characteristics of the church you're leaving. Sincere gratitude or honor from you will both encourage the church as you leave and reinforce your contention that you're following the leading of God. Leaving angry or visibly frustrated once you claim that God is leading you to leave will cast a shadow not only on that contention but also on the process of hearing and responding to God.

Too many people say they are doing God's will but do it in a way that is inconsistent with God's character. This contradiction not only weakens faith, it also corrodes the very notion that a Christian can listen to and be led by God. I don't think people should stop saying that they are being led by God; we should simply say it with more humility (I could be wrong, but as best I understand him right now, I feel led to . . .) and in a way consistent with the character of Jesus. If something we say we are led to do produces only bad fruit (anger, bitterness, slander), it's hard to imagine that God is inspiring it. On the other hand, if what we are led to do produces gratitude, honor and joy, even if the decision isn't the right one, it honors God.

Find ways to thank as many people as you can. It may be that this should be done discreetly because you may not want to draw undue attention to your leaving. Writing cards of appreciation and offering specific and personal thanks to people who have meant something to you is an important part of leaving well.

Follow Through and Leave

After all is said and done, once you have been called to leave, you have to do it. It's possible that in the process of leaving well you experience a kind of renaissance in your relationships in the church. Your attention to the praiseworthy things in the church may generate a kind of nostalgia or a loss of resolve to leave. Leaving will cost you more than you realized. If God has called you to leave, don't lose sight of that; follow through on your decision out of obedience.

Staying at this point would cause confusion. At first such a reversal may be met with positive regard, but in time it will be misunderstood, and when the same issues that led you to leave in the first place resurface for you, which they most certainly will, it will be that much more difficult to leave once you have tried and failed. Trusting God through this process will mean staying the course, even if you forget why you wanted to leave in the first place. Leaving with that much of a positive outlook on the church is the goal. In this way, you can be sure that you're leaving in response to God and not to your own annoyance or frustration.

13

RE-FORMING CHURCH

Some people will leave churches only to look for another one and find that they are again in the same predicament. However, this book, in large part, is for those of us who are tired of that cycle and perhaps have been leavers for some time. What do we do once the leaving is over? Many leavers are confident in their decision, but they feel isolated and alone. Not wanting to go back to church as we know it does not take away the alienation and spiritual ambiguity we can feel. If you're feeling that, I want to reassure you, you're not alone. But you can't stay as you are; you need to begin asking a question: How can we re-form church in our lives?

Remembering the Future

Some have argued that a culture can be defined by its use of language. We are what we say (speech-act theory). Some linguists argue that language's centrality to social activity can't be understated. You can tell a lot about a culture by what they say or, more to the point, by what they don't say. The use of language is the most basic and pervasive form of human interaction. Meaning, of course, is the key. There is nothing significant about the stringing together of arbitrary phonemes to signify something or another. What's important is the meaning of those sounds for the individual or society.

As I think about the emerging church, what will be called

new, I've had to go back to find what we are hungry for. The New Testament church has been an inspiration for every generation. In different ways, every generation finds itself in the story of the first church. However, the church in every era holds lessons and value for us as we think about contextualizing the church for the next generation. As I've thought further about the church, I find myself drawn to old words—words that seem archaic but express something about the future God might be calling us to. I've come to realize that this language is really quite biblical and perhaps its rarity in our usage reflects something about our collective state of mind.

Whatever happened to words like *humility, renunciation, modesty, contrition, self-denial, subjection* and *abasement*? Humility, which was one of the most tangible character traits of Jesus, in its most common derivation, *humiliation*, has come to represent the most heinous and dehumanizing of all acts. To apply the term *nothing* or *nothingness* to oneself is the cardinal sin of psychology. This view, however, was not shared by Abraham (see Genesis 18:27), Job (see Job 19:20), Paul (see 2 Corinthians 12:11), or even Jesus (see John 5:30). Certainly Abraham, Paul and especially Jesus were more than nothing. Yet their willingness to identify with the term is evidence of their thoughts about God, themselves and others. Our unwillingness to do the same also reveals something about us as a culture and about the churches where we learned to speak the language of God. Just as the use of the term reflects their uncompromising humility, which is the secret to the exalted spiritual life, perhaps its absence in our usage reflects our spiritual futility.

As leavers, we have to pray for the grace to shake off the cobwebs of disenchantment and recommit ourselves to the things that really matter. We first have to reenvision church in our hearts, our homes and our relationships. The foundations that have to be laid for re-forming church are ancient ones. Remembering them will mean a revival of ancient words, practices and virtues that until now may have seemed like sermon topics and not real-life concerns. In all our talk about how church should be, we can lose sight of how we should be. Radical churches are composed of radical people. And in the end, it's about collecting virtue and representing love and humility.

Before we re form, we have to remember that the church is Jesus' idea and that it exists to deliver his message and to funnel him glory. We have to remember that the beginning, middle and end of following Jesus is self-denial. Before we re-form as church, we have to be committed to being the kind of people who will build a church not in our own image but in the image of the humble Son of God.

Starting with Ourselves

Jesus said, "If anyone would come after me he must deny himself . . . and follow me" (Matthew 16:24; Mark 8:34; Luke 9:23). Of all the virtues that can be said to represent the Christian life, I want to argue that self-denial will be the most important as we re-form church together. If we move back into worship, community and mission together with a sense of entitlement, bitterness or self-centeredness, we are doomed to fail, and the kind of church we form will not influence change the way it could.

Self-denial acts as a megaphone for the truth. If we are willing to deny ourselves for what is true, the world will notice. If we use the truth only for our gain, who can be expected to believe? It may be that those who preach on television and ask for my money are telling the truth, yet I'm inclined to disbelieve them because of the obvious advantage to them.

In a recent poll, Americans were asked to select the twenty occupations they most admire. In addition, a top-twenty list was compiled resulting in "America's sleaziest ways to make a living." "Television evangelist" appeared third on the second list. The only occupations considered sleazier were "drug dealer" and "organized crime boss." It was more nefarious than "prostitute" and "rock 'n' roll star."

Is there really any wonder why? People will not believe us about the truth of the gospel, or anything else for that matter, if we use it for our own advancement (see 2 Peter 2:13-15). Spiritual opportunism does more harm than good for the gospel and the kingdom of God.

Paul once argued vehemently that those who serve God in the ministry should not have to work and that they are worthy of a salary (see 1 Timothy 5:18). Yet he did not avail himself of that right, simply because he wanted those he served to know that he did it for Jesus and no other reason. His claim to apostleship was never so strong and his ministry was unprecedented because he denied himself and imitated his master. He gave those who had never seen Jesus a life-sized example of what he is like, so much so that he could say under inspiration, "I urge you to imitate me" (1 Corinthians 4:16; see also Galatians 4:12; 2 Thessalonians 3:9). The fact that Paul was whipped, beaten, jailed and constantly under the threat of death is precisely what made his message credible and his motive clear.

Time has passed, but this principle remains the same. The power of the gospel is foolishness to those who are perishing because they chase after worldly power. Their search for immortality is in vain. The way of the gospel is the way of the cross, and for those who come to die, it is life. The paradox proves credible only because the world is looking for what it has been promised but which has never been delivered (except by Jesus): that is, redemption.

Clinging to Discipline

For as long as you remain in the limbo of leaving, you'll need to cling to personal spiritual disciplines. There will be a period for every leaver between the church he has left and the church he hopes to re-form. That can and has lasted years for some of us. Since this isn't the way God intended you to live, it's impossible for you to thrive in this state. However, his grace is still accessible to you, even in the desert of isolation.

The best thing to do in this season is to ruthlessly cling to what you know to do. Many leavers will replace the spiritual input of their former churches with television or radio. In this way, they feel connected to the larger Christian community. But these things are no substitute for personal connection with God and obedience to his voice. As many leavers learn, our spiritual vitality is more than ever related to our personal disciplines. Daily Bible study, prayer, worship, fasting, evangelism, journaling and other disciplines, while important in every believer's life, become paramount for us because they are our only meaningful spiritual input.

Re-forming

How will you re-form church while you have a job, family, responsibilities? You may have the inclination to plant a church, but most will not. It takes a lot of work to form new churches, structure, leadership and all. But being part of the kingdom does take work. Our choice to leave the church can't be a choice to abdicate the Great Commission and our place in it. Here are some ideas for how to go about finding and forming simple churches that minimize bureaucracy and maximize ministry and community.

Build friendships. First realize that you're part of the church. You are still, and perhaps even more so now, released into the broader church. Think of it as being part of a large church. You attend one Sunday school class for some years. After some deliberating, you decide to leave that class and look for another. For a season, while you search, you're released back into the fullness and possibility of all that church has to offer. Your time committed to that one class is now free to be allocated to any ministry in the church. You don't cease to be a part of that church because you left the Sunday school class. In some ways, you're awakened to being more a part of that church.

So it is with leavers. You are released from the particulars of one local congregation to be a part of the body of Christ in your city. Now you have the responsibility to find where you belong in that city and to whom God is calling you into partnership. The time that you have freed up should still be devoted to the kingdom; you now have to enter into a period of exploration, friendship building and networking to find people who are like you or called to the same vision for the church. Leavers should feel invigorated by the fresh air of the church in their cities. There are amazing people to meet and mutually beneficial friendships to engage.

> *The majority of the people that I respect in ministry no longer go to traditional church and they have community that I long for. We have made some steps with some people to try and build some community, but it's difficult at this point.*
>
> DAVE

One way to get out into the kingdom in your city is to look for learning opportunities. Often churches or ministries run conferences, workshops or events meant to enrich the body of Christ in the city. Scout those out. Go to the ones that interest you. If you love music or art, for instance, look for a conference or class on that particular art. While you're there, you can learn, grow, be challenged and make friends.

Keep giving. One of the strange challenges leavers have is what to do with their giving. Many leavers tithed (or came close to tithing) to their local church, and when they leave, that money simply goes unallocated. I want to challenge every leaver not to let disaffection with the church keep you from finding ways to invest in the kingdom. We give out of obedience to God, but we give for other reasons too: Giving is a spiritual benefit to us. When we give, we release some of the pressure of materialism on us and loosen the hold of greed over us. Failure to give only tightens the grip of the most insidious sin in North America. Giving allows us to contribute to things we value but can't participate in directly. Giving is a baseline way to help the poor. I believe we should be committed to more but never less than this basic advocacy for the poor; it's simply too important in Scripture to miss.

Having to find new places to give your money can provide a great opportunity to network with people in your city (and beyond) who are doing heroic things for God. Let people know that you're looking for places to give, and host as many offers as possible. Go to banquets and fundraisers. Be responsible to learn what ministries are doing. Meet the people who are leading and volunteering. You will put yourself in a position both to give responsibly and to meet some great people. God may be calling you into deeper relationship and maybe even to re-form church with some of them.

Serve. I've been stunned by the hypocrisy of some of my own friends (something I see in myself as well) when they leave precisely because the church isn't missional but then fail to engage themselves in meaningful mission after they're gone. We can't criticize the church for flunking mission and then ignore it in our own lives as leavers. Finding places to serve in your city is necessary to preserve your integrity and authenticity, but it's also another excellent way to meet other leavers and people committed to this elusive church practice.

Most cities have independent ministries to at-risk children, the homeless, women in crisis and so on. Having a few hours a week to give in service can open up the city to you in ways previously closed. There are forgotten corners of every city that hold desperate people hungry for genuine care and the message of Jesus. These corners also hold talented, committed believers who might also be looking for a new kind of church.

Third-Place Churches

In their momentous book *The Shaping of Things to Come*, Michael Frost and Alan Hirsch introduce the concept of third-place communities. The idea actually comes from a book called *The Great Good Place* by Ray Oldenburg.

Home, he says, is the first place. First places are, by their very nature, primary in our hearts. Homes are more than houses for us, especially as believers. Our homes are the places where we are most real, most known, most exposed and, I believe, most effective in our witness. To invite nonbelievers into our first place is to invite them into our lives. Having nonbelievers in our homes reminds me of Paul's words in 1 Thessalonians, "We loved you so much that we were delighted to share with you not only the gospel of God but our lives as well" (2:8). In this sense, our homes are great venues to share the gospel as we open all of who we are to those who don't know Jesus. But equally powerful would be the invitation into a nonbeliever's first place, because for her it's also a place of vulnerability and authenticity.

Oldenburg calls work the second place. And while workplaces may provide a great beginning point for witness, they often can be difficult. This leaves the third place. I will let you read a little bit of what Oldenburg writes on the subject:

> Third places exist on neutral ground and serve to level their guests to a condition of social equality. Within these places, conversation is the primary activity and the major vehicle for the display and appreciation of human personality and individuality. Third places are taken for granted and most have a low profile. Since the formal in-

stitutions of society make stronger claims on the individual, third places are normally open in the off hours, as well as at other times. Though a radically different kind of setting from the home, the third place is remarkably similar to a good home in the psychological comfort and support that it extends.

I believe that first and third places need to be our primary points of mission. I would love to see a church defined by its worship, community and mission in first and third places. What we have long called church is really something else entirely and docs not fit into the experience or world of a nonbeliever. As easily as we have formed churches around cathedrals and buildings with steeples and stained glass, we can form churches around pubs and Laundromats, parks and coffee shops. Whole churches may gather in a building for worship and community and then be released into targeted mission. This can work, but why not gather in places of mission and then be released to worship in our homes and other places. In the first church, homes were the place of worship (intimacy with believers, breaking of bread), and their place of gathering was also their place of mission (temple courts). They would gather daily, defining themselves by their third place; the people who went there were the people they hoped to reach with the gospel.

Using Oldenburg's categories opens up two other possibilities for places that simple churches can re-form, what he would call first and third places. Churches have to be able to form wherever believers can gather. For that reason, we have to see that church can form in the most natural and organic places of our lives. Leavers who know other believers in their workplaces need to be empowered to gather people to worship, study the Bible and reach out to their colleagues. God isn't confined to sacred space. In truth, what makes a space sacred is his presence, and his presence is promised to any group who would gather in his name. Marketplace churches will become more common as leavers and other committed believers feel the freedom to gather there in Jesus' name.

The easiest place to re-form church in our lives is in our homes (our first place). These are the places where we are most real, most vulnerable, and where the gospel can be presented in the context of hospitality. Simply, inviting believers and nonbelievers into our homes for the purpose of worshiping and sharing Jesus transforms our homes into churches. You can call it a small group or a cell or whatever makes you comfortable, but if you're worshiping, growing in community and reaching out to the lost and the hurting with the gospel, you are being the church.

Homes are radical places to have church because they're our central place of belonging. They're our sanctuary. Making your home into a place where others can find friendship, healing and the good news of the kingdom is a good place to start for a leaver. Inviting three friends or one other couple is usually enough to start a meeting in your home. It doesn't have to be complicated.

I suggest that you make sure that four elements are present in your home church. First, eat. Sharing a meal is more spiritual than we realize. When we share a meal in memory of Jesus, we proclaim his death until he comes. What we have come to call "communion" means just that. At its simplest level, it's the sharing of a meal with the intention of remembering the body that was broken and the blood that was shed for us. Sharing a simple meal can break down barriers and show love in a basic way.

Second, include the Bible. Don't try to do anything for Jesus without his Word. There are a number of ways you can use the Bible. You don't have to do Bible study. But to keep the emphasis on Jesus and let him define himself, we should integrate the Word into what we do.

Third, invite God's Spirit. There should be an element of openness to the leading of the Holy Spirit. In other words, your time together should not always be the same. There should be some way that God can lead you to do things a little differently from time to time. Maybe that means a time of prayer or an open time of listening. The leaders of the group can think and pray about what unique needs the others might have for that week and what to do about it.

Fourth, the mission. Be sure you have a group of people you hope to reach.

My advice to those of us who long for church that is the kingdom is not to reform the existing church; leave that alone. Instead try to be the church. Pray and serve and organize and dream and plan and give and welcome and sacrifice and form community and have conflict and reconcile and lead and share Jesus and behold and study and pray and teach and baptize and love and be a neighbor and meet needs and know people, all kinds of people. Be the church. Don't be a victim of the structure you were born into; be a leader. Treasure Jesus, know him, study him, and then you will know yourself, who you were meant to be; then you will know the church and what it is meant to be. The vision God has for his bride is the same as the vision he had for his Son. It is the redemption of the world and the ushering in of the kingdom of God.

CONCLUSION
Life After Church

My life after church has become a life after church. What I
thought I was walking away from now haunts my dreams and
stirs my longing heart. God's vision for his church is so magnificent, so beautiful, that we can never leave it without leaving him. Yet we are weak, and I'm a corruption to every ideal
I've ever tried to embody. So I live in the paradox of wanting a
kind of church that I believe God wants, trying not to settle for
less, while at the same time living a merciful life, asking for
and extending mercy to my community when we fail to be what
God has called us to be. Life after church brings us full circle,
back to the need for each other, for God, and for meaning and
purpose. All this is still available for us. But we have to take responsibility for it.

Every generation of believers has to be committed to seeing
the kingdom revealed in its generation. That does not mean we
disparage the way God expressed himself in the generations
before us. On the contrary, the challenge is to hold onto what
we have learned and press forward in the challenge of our current context. In one sense, there's nothing new under the sun.
There's nothing this generation will discover about God or experience that God has not already shown a previous generation of believers. But, on the other hand, no generation of
Christians has ever lived in this time, in this mosaic of culture.

There are similarities, but this time and this church is unique.

Each living generation has to see that it's responsible for its time. God gives spiritual authority to his people to proclaim his kingdom in certain places—among friends or a family or throughout a city block. Generations are given authority over epochs as well.

This is our time. We have been charged with its steward-ship. Ours is the culmination of previous generations. We aren't simply repeating what others have done or following spiritual trends. We have to realize that who God has created us to be is for this time, and we have to live for him in our time.

Great innovators have always been leavers. They aren't re-membered for what they walked away from, but for what they built. In the current church are men and women who left the church of their parents to re-form a new kind of church for their generation. People like Chuck Smith, John Wimber and Bill Hybels left one construction of church to form a new one. Each had a heart to better reach his generation. The results of those movements are nothing short of staggering. Calvary Chapel has planted hundreds of churches all over the world and brought an emphasis on expositional preaching, come-as-you-are, down-to-earth worship and a low-key approach to money. John Wimber and the Vineyard made the Holy Spirit and the charismatic experience of God understandable to a generation of people who didn't grow up in church. And there's barely a church in America that hasn't wrestled with Willow Creek's devotion to seekers and its prophetic emphasis on evangelism.

In their time, these movements and many others have re-shaped the landscape of the church in our nation and around the world. Their contribution is indelibly etched into our minds and hearts. But what now? What will my generation do?

We bless and embrace their contributions while we long for more. We long for churches that are more organic and less franchised. Everyone is not the same and everyone is not called simply to open a small-group franchise for the mother church. Megachurches are powerful, but why are they mostly mono-ethnic? How can we form churches that include people who are different from us? We love the commitment to evangelism, but what about the poor? Jesus' clear emphasis was on the lost and the poor. Why have so many churches built neocathedrals while the poor of the earth suffer the violence of our financial, spiritual and emotional indifference? We are bombarded by the financial demands of the church and we can raise billions for building campaigns, but rarely do we hear from pulpits about the life-and-death needs of war- and famine-wracked lands. Can the church be more global, living out its radical call to remember the poor locally and translocally?

All we have are questions, because the next generation of church has yet to be determined. I want to make a prophetic call to entrepreneurs, those with apostolic gifts, and innova-tors to do your thing. If you have a dream of starting an agency that meets some need or forming a group to chase a purpose that God has planted in your heart, do it. Do not wait. Begin praying, then planning and acting to make that reality. We need activists to arise in this generation.

This is the central purpose of the Underground Network. Our paradigm is that there is no paradigm. We believe that each individual is called into community and that those com-munities are known, called and given authority by God to do something in the world. His mission is translated into the lan-guage of who we are and the needs that we see around us. We want to mobilize as many missional communities as we possi-bly can to determine and then engage their slice of the mission of God, to see the kingdom of God come.

Our brand of church may be more loosely constructed. It may be harder to control. It may be harder to define. Our con-tribution will not be clear mission statements or alignment with one person's ideas of what everyone ought to do. We hope to stimulate as many believers as we can to seek out community and to learn to hear God on their own for their unique contribution—what it is and how to do it. We believe that in every city are gaps in the coverage of the kingdom, and we want to inspire as many communities as we can to discern a gap and begin to lovingly engage it.

Go get 'em, leavers. Find a new identity in what we are called to build. Bind yourselves together. Pick your battles and care about the kingdom first.

Jesus is coming soon.

A LEAVER'S MANIFESTO
Our Lucid Hope Revisited

I've shared ideas about life after church with many people who seem to experience a deep resonance with certain ideas about the church they hope for. This vision is my own waking dream—and the dream of many others—of what the church can be.

The People of God

The centrality of the Lord's Supper. The celebration of the Lord's Supper was meant to be more regular and less symbolic than is currently practiced. Through the breaking of bread, the early church was built, and it's around the table that Jesus insisted he should be remembered. In the context of a shared meal, the breaking of bread and sharing of the cup also serves to forge the community of redeemed sinners while also placing the theology of the cross at the center of all theory and practice.

The model of team leadership. The single-leader church has to go. It's not only unhealthy for the lone leader (and the community being led), but it also limits the work of the Holy Spirit. Single-leader churches expect the gifts of the whole body to be evident in one leader. This is both unrealistic and unhealthy. The Holy Spirit gives gifts to all for the building of the body, which should never be restricted or encumbered by the monopoly of the one. Because Jesus appointed a team of leaders over the first church, and they in turn also appointed leaders as a team (people who were known to be full of the Holy Spirit), it stands to reason that the contemporary church should also be led by a team of trusted and reputable leaders. This structure is not only biblical, but it also affords leaders more accountability and less pressure, more creativity and less error, more gifts used for the church and less one-dimensional teaching, more of the Bible with fewer blind spots, more faith, more prayer and more joy.

The representation of multiethnicity. The church has to be the vanguard in racial reconciliation by addressing the sin and structures of racism, both in society and in the church at large. This is done in part by valuing and including all ethnic groups and by making sure our worship and the expression of our faith is unbiased, relevant and crosscultural. It isn't enough to simply be *willing* to be a multiethnic church; the leaders of the church must labor to achieve this critical feature of the ecclesial vision and build a church that represents the ethnic diversity of their specific city. In so doing, we live the Lord's Prayer that his kingdom would be on earth as it is in heaven.

The implementation of spiritual gifts. The church has to allow all its people to discover and use their spiritual gifts, thus fulfilling them individually and expanding the breadth and depth of ministry done by the church collectively. We have to allow teachers to teach, prophets to prophesy, leaders to lead, administrators to administrate and so on. Also, the free movement of the Spirit and the expression of charismatic gifts has to be both valued and expected, as we allow the supernatural manifestation of God's leadership into all we do.

The priesthood of all believers. The church has to call all believers into leadership and service within the church. Until Jesus returns, it's the vocation of all of Christ's followers to labor for the kingdom and to serve in the church. While some may be set apart for full-time service and leadership, all believers are called to the same cause and all labor to that end. Therefore one of the church's primary responsibilities is to equip the saints for acts of service, to train, empower and support believers as they lead and serve.

The Word of God

The centrality of Scripture. The whole Bible has to be central to the life of the church. It should be the focus of all sustained study and discussion, and it should define our understanding of ourselves and the world around us. The Bible must be systematically taught, so that parts aren't excluded due to a lack of understanding or a failure in the theology of a particular teacher. All teachers should be held to a high standard of accurate and faithful hermeneutics so that the Scriptures are studied, taught and understood literally while also being appreciated in the light of relevant pretext, subtext and context.

The process of disciple-making. People have to be taught to fend for themselves spiritually. The role and goal of teaching should be to empower people to think critically and to hear from God on their own. Since there is only one God and one mediator between God and man, church leaders can never become the only source of divine direction for believers. Instead our task is to teach people to become deeper disciples of Jesus by learning how to use Scripture to hear God and, in turn, to disciple others to do likewise.

The method of application. Learning has to be active. People have to be convinced that something is learned only when it's practiced. We have to call people to live out the Scriptures in accountable, disciple-making relationships.

The Mission of God

The principle of expansion. We hope to build on the principle of expansion. The goal of the church is the expansion of the

kingdom. We dream and labor to increase the reign of the Lord
Jesus on earth and to join him in building his kingdom. We do
this by increasing the depth of our own submission to his will
and by including more and more people into his family. The
goal, then, is always to multiply and include more people.
Thus, change itself is a constant and is to be desired because
it's related to growth.

The necessity of evangelism. We dream of a church that does not
grow too sophisticated for evangelism. We want to keep the making of disciples as the primary and preferred mode of expansion—including more and more people in our home churches as
we include more and more people in the kingdom of God.

Embracing the whole gospel. We want to be the kind of church
that always proclaims and lives the whole gospel, and embraces the paradoxes—justice and evangelism, grace and judgment, the call to suffering and the promise of joy, and so on.

Prayer. We hope for a church that is committed to night-
and-day prayer for the world and for a deeper revelation of
God. Without prayer, the church becomes disconnected from
the work of the Spirit, and independence from God, not dependence on God, is fostered.

The Kingdom of God

Doing justice. We dream of a church that takes a prophetic
stand against all kinds of evil, not only spiritual but also soci-
etal. All sin and injustice is the enemy of the church and the
kingdom of God. In word and in deed, the church has to begin
with itself by confronting the sin of materialism and the hoard-
ing of wealth at the expense of the poor. Not only should the
church be a voice against injustice and the subjugation of the
poor in the world, but it should also act to free people from
the yoke of oppression through sacrifice for and solidarity
with the poor. This is done in part, but is not limited to, the
allocation of church resources.

The truth about giving. In turn, the church we want will teach the truth about giving in the context of global poverty. We long to teach the overwhelming biblical theme of responsibility for the poor in general and the suffering church in particular. We have to call people, not to the tithe (which is a lesser doctrine superseded by the new covenant), but to giving all of themselves to God, surrendering all of their resources to the bidding of the Lord Jesus. We have to teach people that this means giving sacrificially to the needs of others and the spread of the gospel around the world. The church should be sure to take care of each other's needs by sharing all that we have and by giving excessively, at least half of all that is given, to the poor and the cause of missions around the world.

The quality of simplicity. We dream of a church that's committed to spending as little as possible on herself and to eliminating frivolous expenses, because she sees that we are part of the larger body of Christ around the world that suffers in want, with basic needs superseding our desires for luxury. This way there will always be the prioritizing of need based on a global view of the church and the resources of God's people—not on the myopic desires of the local church alone.

The building block of the home church. We must call people to integrate Christianity into all parts of their lives. We have to reject the practice of containing spirituality to a building or a two-hour block on Sunday morning. We have to bring the church into our neighborhoods and into our homes. We have to demystify the word *church* by bringing it into focus. We have to call people to share their lives by making their homes, every small gathering and even every relationship a sanctuary where God can be worshiped.

Homes provide the context for the sharing of pain, joy, resources and gifts, as well as kinetic teaching of the Word through dialogue, inquiry and the remembrance of the cross at every meal. The larger gathering of home churches together has to be seen as special (a good thing) but not church. In the larger setting, worship and celebration, teaching and learning will happen, but unless there is also the nurture and development of genuine community (where people's lives are shared) we aren't being the church. That can fully happen only when we gather in settings where we are known and can share and grow together. Church has to be based on authentic relationship. By definition, anonymity cannot be a characteristic of the church. We can affirm the larger gathering for worship and celebration, but we can't call it church.

NOTES

page 19   Leaving is a stage: Alan Jamieson, *A Churchless Faith: Faith Journeys Beyond the Churches* (London: SPCK, 2002), pp. 39, 107.

page 24   He also recorded: William D. Hendricks, *Exit Interviews* (Chicago: Moody Press, 1993), p. 20.

page 35   He argues: Dave Tomlinson, *The Post-Evangelical*, rev. ed. (El Cajon, Calif.: Emergent YS/Zondervan, 2003), p. 3.

page 36   In his book: Alan Jamieson, *A Churchless Faith: Faith Journeys Beyond the Churches* (London: SPCK, 2002), p. 109.

page 36   [Leavers] also frequently claim: John Drane, *The McDonaldization of the Church: Consumer Culture and the Church's Future* (Macon, Ga.: Smyth & Helwys, 2003), p. 5.

page 45   As more people seek: Michael Moynagh, *Changing World, Changing Church* (London: Monarch, 2001), pp. 74-75.

page 51   Reality is no longer: Tomlinson, *Post-Evangelical*, p. 79.

page 52   The earliest Christian: Vinoth Ramachandra, *The Recovery of Mission: Beyond the Pluralist Paradigm* (Grand Rapids: Eerdmans, 1997), p. 226.

pages 52-53   The task facing: Eddie Gibbs, *ChurchNext: Quantum Changes in How We Do Ministry* (Downers Grove, Ill.: InterVarsity Press, 2000), p. 212.

page 59   It was like: At first glance, you see a woman looking at the sea, along with other smaller pictures, but if you back up far enough or take your eyes out of focus, you see Abraham Lincoln's head.

page 167   Some have argued: Jonathan Potter and Margaret
              Wetherell, *Discourse and Social Psychology: Beyond Atti-
              tudes and Behavior* (Newbury Park, Calif.: Sage, 1987),
              p. 14.

page 169   In a recent poll: James Patterson and Peter Kim, *The
              Day America Told the Truth* (New York: Prentice Hall,
              1991), p. 144.

page 174   Third places exist: Ray Oldenburg, *The Great Good
              Place: Cafés, Coffee Shops, Community Centers, Beauty
              Parlors, General Stores, Bars, Hangouts, and How They
              Get You Through the Day* (New York: Paragon House,
              1991), p. 86.

SCRIPTURE INDEX

A man comes across an ancient enemy, beaten and left for dead. He lifts the wounded man onto the back of a donkey and takes him to an inn to tend to the man's recovery. Jesus tells this story and instructs those who are listening to "go and do likewise."

Likewise books explore a compassionate, active faith lived out in real time. When we're skeptical about the status quo, Likewise books challenge us to create culture responsibly. When we're confused about who we are and what we're supposed to be doing, Likewise books help us listen for God's voice. When we're discouraged by the troubled world we've inherited, Likewise books encourage us to hold onto hope.

In this life we will face challenges that demand our response. Likewise books face those challenges with us so we can act on faith.

LIKEWISE.   *Go and do.*

likewisebooks.com